BLEED AND SEE

Chris Laoutaris

Author royalties from the sales of Bleed and See will go directly to Carers UK. As the UK's only national membership charity for carers, Carers UK is both a supportive community and a movement for change.

https://www.carersuk.org/

in support of

carersUK

ISBN: 978-1-915079-90-9

'Bloodflower' cover art, page 1 'Aurum Lily' illustration, and final 'Flower Study' illustration by: George Laoutaris

Cover designed by Aaron Kent

Edited and typeset by Aaron Kent

Broken Sleep Books
Rhydwen,
Talgarreg,
Ceredigion
SA44 4HB

Broken Sleep Books
Fair View
St Austell
Cornwall
PL26 7YH

This is a courageous, moving and deeply moral collection, as endlessly curious and outward looking as it is intellectually generous and compassionate. In Laoutaris we have a poet who invites us to think deeply, radically, and rewards us with imagistic genius and indelible phrasing. And unflinching and clear-sighted. Any serious poet is probably haunted by Adorno's charge, a sense of its impossibility, or to stand outside the hall of mirrors we're duty-bound to critique; it moves me to read work which achieves that. *Bleed and See* is a character study (for all of us as well as its subject, the poet's brother George), an elegy, a profound literary and ontological history. A vital debut.
— Luke Kennard, Winner of the Forward Prize for Poetry for *Notes on the Sonnets*

In *Bleed and See* Laoutaris shows how difference becomes the pretext for the dehumanizing of the other, of how we relish standing taller than, cutting off at the knees, those we "see" as different and those we are blindly taught to fear. Every poem speaks not just to one brother's experiences, to the inhumanity suffered by the individual, but to the larger worldwide inhumanity we perpetuate against our common humanity. The 'brother' of these poetic psalms is as much our brother in love and pain as he is the poet's. Laoutaris is an incredible writer, the bearer of deep-evoking truths which stir change wherever the winds of his words touch wounds.
— Neal Hall, MD, Winner of the Black Caucus of the American Library Association Best Poetry Book Award

'The odds of flesh and fang which meet in the fabric.' Chris Laoutaris' poems manage to turn visceral suffering into something sacred: a set of finely wrought objects we turn over and over as we encounter the difficult fact of living with disability. His poems offer complex forms of material anthropology — a mesmerising dance macabre. Laoutaris reminds us that art can be wrought from the ugliness of pain, and that poetic metaphor, when it is so carefully curated, can produce sudden and startling releases of feeling. Exquisite relief.

Bleed and See is reminiscent of the poetry of Jacobean revenge drama - Webster's *The Duchess of Malfi* and *The White Devil* - run through the idioms of twentieth century lyrical poets Sylvia Plath and Robert Lowell. His poems explode in front of us but their effect is often a deadly quiet: the quiet sound of love feeling its way through depths of pain.
— Sally Bayley, author of *Girl With Dove* and *No Boys Play Here*

Also by Chris Laoutaris

Shakespeare's Book: *The Intertwined Lives Behind the First Folio*
(William Collins, 2023)

Shakespeare and the Countess: The Battle that Gave Birth to the Globe
(Penguin Books, 2014)

Shakespearean Maternities: Crises of Conception in Early Modern England
(Edinburgh University Press, 2008)

Contents

Bleed and See

Chris Laoutaris

'Black Rose', self-Portrait by George Laoutaris

Preparatory studies for 'Black Rose', self-portraits by George Laoutaris

'Black Rose' is a self-portrait produced by my brother, George, after he started displaying symptoms of the neurological illness that would end his life prematurely. He created a series of 'draft' studies (two of which are shown above) as preparatory images for the main work. He was in his mid-to-late teens when he crafted these paintings, which deal not only with the onset of his paralysing terminal illness but with the effects of a long-term skin-disfiguring condition (not presented directly in these self-portraits) which led to his sense of alienation and ostracization. This is expressed through the muted tones with which he has rendered himself in two of these paintings, and the black rose which represents his burdened heart. But there is also hope encoded within these images. The vibrant flowers, their revelation of the resilience of nature, and the crucifix promise renewal and resurrection through suffering. In a note on the portrait my brother explained that 'the rose has a strong stem… symbolising my strength of character'. This strength was a trait he demonstrated throughout the challenges he faced with his disfigurement and long-term disability, and *Bleed and See* is an attempt to capture something of the emotional complexities of his difficult journey and of my role as his carer.

The cover art for this book, entitled 'Bloodflower', combines one of the flowers my brother painted for the 'Black Rose' self-portrait with Aaron Kent's powerful symbolic rendering of the bleeding 'stigmata'. I wanted the image to be placed over a canvas background in acknowledgement of the book's theme and my brother's love for his art. The cover encapsulates so much of the core message of *Bleed and See*: the wisdom acquired through suffering is a kind of gift which, when communicated honestly, can be the source of comfort, healing, and restoration for ourselves and others, often in ways we cannot anticipate.

For my brother George
The truer seer

And for our parents John and Thalia
For the eternities in all they have gifted to us

But none can tell, if you be well, nor where you doo sojurne:
Which makes me feare, that I shall heare your health appaired is:
And oft I dream, that you are dead, or somthyng goeth amys.
Yet when I thinke, you can not shrinke, but must with Maister bee:
I have good hope, when you have scope, you wyll repaire to mee.
And so the feare, and deepe dispaire, that I of you then had
I dryve away: and wysh that day wherin we may be glad....
As you shall know, for I wyll show, you more when we doo speake,
Then wyll I wryt, or yet resyte, within this Paper weake.

— Isabella Whitney, 'To her Brother. B.W.', from *A Sweet Nosgay*, 1573

...all this to season
A brother's dead love...

— William Shakespeare, *Twelfth Night*, 1.1.29-30

Introduction

Refiguring Disfigurement and Disability: An Essay on Critical Poetics

Evey single poem in *Bleed and See* is about the same subject: my brother, George. Most of the collection incorporates what might be termed my *juvenilia* and responds to his battles with long-term disfigurement and subsequent disability after being diagnosed with a progressive neurological illness which led to his early death. I submitted the core of this work for the Eric Gregory Poetry Awards shortly before George's passing and it was shortlisted for the prize. Not long after, I expanded the collection and revised some of the poems, returning to them occasionally and making small changes in the succeeding years. The majority, however, are as I had written them: raw, uncensored and immediate reactions to his conditions, my role as his carer over a nearly fifteen-year period, and his untimely loss. Since then I have had numerous opportunities to publish the volume. I turned down the offer every time.

But why didn't I publish these poems? Was it because they were intensely personal, written largely in the moment, and I had therefore come to view them as too visceral, unrefined, too emotional even, going against the grain of what I like to think of as my habitually even-handed and stable temperament? Or was it due to the fact that they dealt with something which was quite difficult to quantify: what it meant to be a long-term carer for someone with a chronic degenerative illness? Or did my attempts to capture my brother's reactions to his own disfigurement and disability make me feel uncomfortable because they reflected the *wrong* kind of emotions? These poems are, for the most part, unsentimental, refusing to represent my brother in ways which fit socially prescribed views of how those with disabilities are *supposed* to be presented: meek, long-suffering, resilient paragons of virtue, archetypes for our own salvation.

Do not misunderstand me. My brother was all those things, at different times, and faced every trial with astonishing courage and grace; with patience, charitable generosity in his dealings with others, and with an undimmed capacity to love, despite his suffering. But he was so much more. The portraits of my brother which emerge from this collection record an individual who is also complex and sometimes deeply troubled. George had suffered horrendous bullying, both within the school system and outside it, as a consequence of a skin-disfiguring condition. This was succeeded, or rather overlapped with, a neurological illness, diagnosed in his late teens, which cut short his ambition to become a painter (he was something of a prodigy as a child; at least he was so viewed by those who witnessed his quickly-developing artistic skill) and would, it soon became clear, cut short his life. Within a year of diagnosis he had begun to lose his eyesight, the use of his limbs, and many of his bodily functions. Not only had he seen the darker side of human nature, as the subject of public curiosity, prejudice and aggression, but was fast losing his independence and his hopes for the future, experiencing his incredible talents slipping through his grasp before he had started to realise his full potential. He had also found himself in an alien world, one designed for the able-bodied, which seemed in its very fabric to confirm his body as other, as ill-suited to its environment, as the exception rather than the rule. As a result he could be angry, unforgiving, furious with life, misanthropic, and given to bouts of depression and deep anxiety.

Despite the Eric Gregory Award shortlisting, when I surveyed these poems I seemed to say to myself: *No, this is not the collection you should have written. It should have been tender, sentimental, poignant; full of a kind of nostalgic aesthetic delicacy which erased, with a deftness and lightness of touch which became paradoxically heroic in its aims, these darker experiences. That's what a 'real' poet would have done.* But this is not what I, or my brother, were experiencing at the time. A teenager myself, I had become my older brother's carer, and had to watch his body fail him, witness the gradual loss of his ability to fulfil the talent which I had so urgently wanted him to express. None of this was pretty. I felt that in publishing the remnants of those experiences I might be doing a disservice to other people with disabilities, or with chronic or terminal illnesses, and their carers or loved ones. So anxious was I about this that I had determined not to publish the collection.

I was not then equipped critically to evaluate my own feelings. Only very recently, after delving more deeply into critical disability studies as a concerted discipline, have I begun to acquire the tools to understand that my discomfort with publishing these poems stemmed from social expectations and culturally engrained ideologies which derived from specific historical determinants which shaped the representation of those with disfigurements and disabilities in very particular ways. My studies showed me that non-normative individuals in the media, in art, in literature, and in other artefacts of the culture, are often leached of their complexity, of their *total* humanity. In writing these poems I had been, without then realising it, searching for the authentic *completeness* which was missing in the portrayals of disfigurement and disability I had imbibed and which became the spectres against which I was measuring my own writing. I have come to realise that publishing these now is a way of laying those ghosts to rest, of resisting their suasive and deluding voices. In this critical introduction I will outline some of my own discoveries in the journey towards this realisation and reflect on the ways in which they have changed my understanding of these poems, written in difficult times so long ago, but which still resonate with an ever-presence which makes them part of an on-going process, one which, I hope, stands as a tribute to my brother, George, and which ultimately expresses how much his life is a perpetual gift to me and our parents, even years after his death.

'a penny to view': Cultures of Seeing

Do we really *see* people with disfigurements and disabilities? Are we afraid to look? After all, it is rude to stare. A simple stare can signify in so many ways. And signification *is* action. A stare can endorse, validate, or be weaponised to hurt, humiliate and demolish. It is hardly surprising that, when it comes to non-normative bodies, in a public forum at least, not staring is the default stance. In their book, *Recovering Disability in Early Modern England*, Allison P. Hobgood and David Houston Wood affirm that engaging with 'Disability studies… reveals how these "insufficient" bodies and persons, paradoxically, are made less visible the more they demand notice'.[1] A solution to this potentially effacing invisibility is to cultivate a critical discourse which:

> …prods us to stare differently at disability, disability histories, and disability representations. It mandates that we stop refusing to look or that we, equally problematically, cease gawking unilaterally at the extraordinary; instead, it proposes engagement in a reciprocal interaction in which disability, disability histories, and disability representations stare back. This reciprocity and mutual recognition may cause unease in readers, but such is the price, and ultimate advantage, of ethical staring encounters.[2]

This 'staring back' – an inter-*active* and reciprocal exchange of glances – was precisely the keynote on which I began *Bleed and See* and which I wanted to resonate across the collection as a whole. The first poem, 'Human Skin', reflects on a series of arresting wall-portraits by Vasiliki Gkotsi of individuals with facial deformities, disfigurements and skin-conditions who stare back at the viewer.

1 Allison P. Hobgood and David Houston Wood, *Recovering Disability in Early Modern England* (Ohio State University Press, 2013), p. 3.
2 Hobgood and Wood, *Recovering Disability in Early Modern England*, p. 2.

Defiant, confrontational, interrogatory, they demand to be seen. Pasted directly onto the gallery's exposed brickwork, these portraits blend with the imperfections, cracks and anomalies of the walls they adorn. The effect is heart-stopping and, yes, beautiful. These fearless faces spoke to my own experience of my brother's condition and represented what I wanted the collection, in part, to achieve; a challenging of the supposed victimhood created by *one-way* acts of seeing when directed at the individual with a disfigurement or disability:

> He is no more a victim than I.
> He is aware of his deformity
> and is confronting us with it.
>
> ... You must
> have asked if these are cracks
> in brick-work or merely clumps
>
> of scarred tissue; a step back
> and the wrack and sable of this face,
> in its imperishable contours,
> will show he is our instigator...
>
> ...Learned connoisseurs,
>
> (for you have come to judge
> each peek and grimace of my art),
> quantify the way this image
> meddles with our certainty of love... ('Human Skin')

I wanted to capture the possibilities of the confrontational glance; the subject of the apparently 'extraordinary' or 'unfamiliar' body staring back, with equal potential to judge, to evaluate, to discern, to discriminate, to play the connoisseur. The 'unease' which Hobgood and Wood identify as the outcome of such a 'staring encounter' is an essential precursor to the 'mutual recognition' which dissolves an alienating *otherness*. Lennard J. Davis, in his book *Bending over Backwards: Disability, Dismodernism, and Other Difficult Positions*, takes this a stage further by arguing for a 'dismodernist ethics' which recognises that 'the by now outdated postmodern subject is a ruse to disguise the hegemony of normalcy'. In contrast, the 'dismodernist subject is in fact disabled', and therefore it follows that '*all* humans are seen as wounded' since 'impairment is the rule, and normalcy is the fantasy. Dependence is the reality, and independence grandiose thinking'. For Davis, disability discourses which locate prejudice within the visual exceptionalism of the 'different' body appropriate 'somatic markers... as a device to distract us from the unity of new ways of regarding humans and their bodies'. The implication is that these new ways of seeing have been, are being, obfuscated by 'Disability scholars' who widen the gap between normal and 'nonstandard' bodies through a discourse of 'ableism' which 'locate[s] that distance in social constructions such as "the stare," that telling glance directed towards people with physical differences'. As such 'the stare' is reconstituted as a narrative 'device' which shores up an already dying postmodern subject whose renewal as a 'dismodern' citizen depends on a recognition that we all possess 'nonstandard' bodies.[3] Although I endorse the call for a shared empathy which underpins this approach, I find it much harder to efface the potentially tyrannous and destructive power of the (one-way) stare beneath a pleasantly universalising idea of a common disability. It just seems too easy.

While Davis is not alone in seeking to, in the words of Hobgood and Wood, find a path towards a form of 'radical inclusivity' through critical approaches to disability which embrace the concept of the atypical subject as the norm, I have found this did not quite match my own experience.[4] The stare my brother's stare repeatedly encountered seemed to confirm not a shared universal state but a radical 'difference'. In one instance – one of many I could have chosen to illustrate this point – my brother had been accosted on the bus by a young woman and her friends who laughed conspicuously at him and engaged in

3 Lennard J. Davis, *Bending over Backwards: Disability, Dismodernism, and Other Difficult Positions* (New York and London: New York University Press, 2002), pp. 30-35.

4 Hobgood and Wood, *Recovering Disability in Early Modern England*, p. 6.

theatrical whispering, all the while fixing him with their unwavering and curious stares. When he asked them if they were laughing at him she, their apparent ring-leader, affirmed that they were. When he suggested she think about how she would feel if she had his condition and was the subject of strangers' laughter, her response was this casual statement: 'If I looked like you, I would commit suicide.' Such a reaction, whatever insecurities it covered, seemed to me to be freighted with premises which it should alarm us to see internalised in anyone, let alone someone so young: *I am normal; you are deviant. I am beauty; you are monster. I am right; you are wrong. I have a right to life; you do not.* Far from our postmodern condition being one which collapses or transcends 'identity politics', my participation in the, sometimes explosive, drama of others' encounters with my brother's body seemed to confirm a body-rooted 'identity' as a site of contest, assault, offense and defence in a manner expressed succinctly by Rosemarie Garland Thomson in her *Extraordinary Bodies: Figuring Physical Disability in American Culture and Literature*:

> Corporeal departures from dominant expectations never go uninterpreted or unpunished, and conformities are almost always rewarded. The narrative of deviance surrounding bodies considered different is paralleled by a narrative of universality surrounding bodies that correspond to notions of the ordinary or the superlative... In this economy of visual difference, those bodies deemed inferior become spectacles of otherness while the unmarked are sheltered in the neutral space of normalcy. Invested with meanings that far outstrip their biological bases, figures such as the cripple, the quadroon, the queer, the outsider, the whore are taxonimical, ideological products marked by socially determined stigmata, defined through representation, and excluded from social power and status.[5]

The disabled, non-normative, disfigured, or 'extraordinary' body must first be *seen* to be 'interpreted', to be judged, whether through physical 'stigmata' or through nonstandard behaviours. It must be seen to bleed. But what is apparent to sight is not really the body itself, in its

5 Rosemarie Garland Thomson, *Extraordinary Bodies: Figuring Physical Disability in American Culture and Literature* (New York: Columbia University Press, 1997), pp. 7-8.

present materiality. That body is, rather, seen *through* layers of body-defining histories, of what I regard as *cultures of seeing*, informed by the development of the taxonomical sciences, the discoveries of anatomy, the discourses of wonder, curiosity and magic, and the fascination with the monstrous figure, which determine the markers of deviancy and abnormality against which the 'normal' receives its confirmation and validation.[6] Making this apparent had, in fact, always been the intent (though I did not then have the framework I do now to make this speak to a broader context of critical and creative disability studies) behind the two-part structure of *Bleed and See*. Part 1, 'Alien Arcana', explores these cultures of seeing in history and was prompted by a question I had often asked myself every time my brother was pointed at, pointed out, stared at, laughed at, cursed, aggressively accosted, or even simply regarded with curiosity, pity or sympathy: what made my brother such a wonder?

The answer for me lay in the ever-rippling resonance of these body-histories and their attendant cultures of seeing: the freak show; the cabinet of wonders; the so-called 'monstrous birth' and the development of the teratological sciences; the uncanny and uncannily connected bodies of witches and their bewitched victims; the corporealising catharsis of ancient sacrificial and burial rituals; the western fascination with Greek and Egyptian art; the physicalising poetics of the prophet or seer; and the fantasy that cloning, genetic engineering and other cybernetic technologies will provide ways of refining and 'perfecting' the human subject. I encounter these complex and often intertwining histories in the first section of this collection, confronting the place of the non-normative body – the body in crisis, the body deformed,

6 In my first monograph *Shakespearean Maternities: Crises of Conception in Early Modern England* (Edinburgh: Edinburgh University Press, 2008), I explored these very 'body-defining histories' and the ways in which they contributed to the material, literary and visual cultures which were the foundations for today's body-prejudices. For a fascinating account of the ways in which the 'normal' body is constructed at the intersection between the development of the disciplines of anatomy and cartography, explored through a Shakespearean lens, see Valerie Traub, 'The Nature of Norms in Early Modern England: Anatomy, Cartography, *King Lear*', *South Central Review*, Vol. 26, No. 1/2 (2009), pp. 42-81. For a valuable historical study of disability in the Tudor period see Phillipa Vincent-Connolly's *Disability and the Tudors: All the King's Fools* (Yorkshire: Pen & Sword, 2021).

the body fragmenting yet defiantly whole, the extraordinary or unfamiliar body, the body disabled and dis-abled, the body in the process of being constructed by nascent scientific endeavours – in art, ritual, myth, medical setting, and literary construction. But every one of those bodies is also the body of my brother, because I came to realise that others' encounters with his body was a *seeing through* those layered corporealities in a manner which determined what exactly was *seen*. The jolt for me – every single time – was that this was not who I was seeing. This was not George.

How do I account for this – to re-appropriate Lennard J. Davis' term – 'distance' in perception? And was I obliged to do anything about it? Was this part of my responsibility as my brother's 'carer'? Throughout writing most of the collection I was a postgraduate student at University College London, studying Shakespeare and Renaissance Literature, then subsequently an early career researcher and British Academy Post-Doctoral Fellow. No surprise then that the fruits of my literary and historical studies were what I turned to in trying to make sense of this. It had been obvious to me how far both science and superstition had conspired in the creation of a relentlessly fictionalised, narrativised, and moralised non-normative body. The culture which produced widely circulated cheap broadside ballads defining children born with congenital abnormalities, disfigurements or disabilities as 'monstrous births' – in one instance presenting such a child as a divine warning of the punishments awaiting England for its 'monstrous vice' and, in another example, revealing how 'grossest faults burst out in body's form/And monster... shows the sea of sin whose storm/Overflows and [over]whelms virtue's barren shore'[7] – is the same which saw Sir Francis Bacon insist on the serious inductive study of '*Deviating Instances*; that is, errors, vagaries and prodigies of nature, wherein nature deviates and turns aside from her ordinary course'. Bacon emphasised the need to 'make a collection or particular natural history of all prodigies and monstrous births of nature; of everything in short that is in nature new, rare, and unusual', his belief being that 'nature', if 'detected in her deviation', could be corrected, perfected, leading her back by art to the point whither she strayed by

7 These ballads are part of the British Library's Huth Ballads collection: *The Forme and Shape of a Monstrous Childe, borne at Maydstone in Kent* (1568); *The true report of the forme and shape of a monstrous childe, borne at Muche Horkesleye* (1562).

accident'.[8] Either end of this polarity is disturbing. The 'deviant' body is a revelation of humanity's moral and spiritual degradation, a *monster* in the literal sense – in its relation to the root meaning of the Latin *monstrum*, indicating a portent or sign, which derives from *monere*, indicating the process of reminding, bringing to one's forethought, teaching or warning; from whence we derive the word 'demonstrate', which discloses the ocular power inherent in the pedagogical display of the monster – or it is an 'accident', a freak of nature, which must be corrected.

The cultures of seeing which produced both these polarities are woven through the 'Alien Arcana' section of *Bleed and See*; from the images of such prodigies as 'a four-legged chick, a two-headed rat,/a baby's face on a calabash' recorded by the society of learning known as the Lincean Academy (its proponents themselves influenced by the work of Bacon and Galileo) in their investigations into the monstrous anatomies of nature in the poem 'Inhuman Histories', to the curios of a 'pickled baby's hand' and exotic 'baby crocodile' accumulated by the seventeenth-century collector of rarities in the poem 'The Cabinet of Curiosities'. The poem 'Bartholomew Baby', for instance, takes as its premise the early modern version of the freak-show. It emphasises the unnaturalness of the 'distance' which the baby's 'freak' status, as culturally-constituted icon, interposes between mother and son; an *interjecting* framework which short-circuits the natural bond of affection between human beings; or, more precisely, a pluralised multi-layered process of interjecting frameworks, involving the discourses and visual tropes attached to the concepts of wonder, curiosity and witchcraft, which turn the child into a 'monster':

> The 'unlucky bairn',
> curled like a gryllus in a medieval folio,
>
> inhabited the tooled margin of wonder,
> and would be, just as she had once seen

8 Frances Bacon, *Novum Organum, The Works of Francis Bacon,* ed. James Spedding (London: Longman and Co., 1875), Vol. 4, pp. 55 and 168-9.

on the painted board of a Bartholomew Fair,
'Portent of dire wrack, the hammer of God
in our latter times'. Would they one day lay out

a penny to view this witch's changeling
torn from nature's smooth endearments?
The mother's arms will hold a bag of ash.
When the word-gatherers arrive she will know
the world has come between her and her son.
('Bartholomew Baby')

As with 'Human Skin', in which Vasiliki Gkotsi's provocative portraits force us to question the prejudices or expectations which unsettle the 'certainty of love', what is being disturbed here, through the identity-effacing narratives about the non-normative or deviant body, is the natural connection between human beings. What stimulates this disturbance is the point at which a private body becomes *seen*, is displayed and evaluated. The reason why so many poems in the first section of this collection describe exhibitions of one kind or another – in museums, galleries, cabinets, anatomy theatres, archaeological sites, or ritualised contexts – is that the deviant body is so often in our cultures of seeing the exhibiting, or rather exhibited, body (a realisation which my brother himself, as an artist, laboured to get across in his work). But my interest in Shakespeare also meant I could not read characters like Richard III or Caliban without developing a sense that the body as locus of wonder is also a *performative* body. The body-histories on which I drew for these poems are literally *at play* in Richard III's body: 'Cheated of feature by dissembling nature,/Deformed, unfinished… scarce half made up,/ And that so lamely and unfashionable…/And therefore, since I cannot prove a lover…/I am determinèd to prove a villain'.[9] It is apparent from this confession just how readily the performance of 'deformity' is transmuted into monstrosity; it is a script Richard is rehearsing, one infinitely played out in and through the cultures of seeing which

9 William Shakespeare, *Richard III,* 1.1.19-30; *Richard III,* ed. John Jowett (Oxford: Oxford University Press, 2000).

inform his character's creation. But there is also something more complex going on. If Richard's body is a performing body, a body on display, the unsettling power which inheres in his 'staring back' at and 'talking back' to the audience is equally performative. What lies at the root of this uncanny power? Katherine Schaap Williams, in *Unfixable Forms: Disability, Performance, and the Early Modern English Theater*, sees the theatre as a space in which the potential 'monstrosity' of disabled corporeality is performed by 'unfixable' bodies:

> While the promise of viewing a monstrous body at the fairground depends on a claim to singularity ("pay to see what you've never seen before")… [the] stage formally refuses an original, and the theater builds iteration into its practice – every performance is another night, another actor, another production… When a body is described as "monstrous," the logic of repetition that underpins theatrical representation is at odds with the logic of singularity (this body, born in this place, with these specific deformed features) that gives the rhetoric of monstrosity its force in early modern print culture and in the fair's display... At the same time, because no performance ever happens the same way twice, the theater offers a monster that is uniquely singular because it is temporary, produced at the intersection of actor's body and monstriferous properties. The iterative work that constitutes early modern theatrical practice demonstrates that the monster is always made up, fixing an actor's body through the power of theatrical prosthetics, and unfixing the monster's alterity in the process.[10]

I find this a very useful way of thinking about the power of poetry. Poetry *voices* the non-normative body and in its 'unfixedness' can unsettle preconceptions and challenge, by confronting, the images of that body created by the cultures of seeing of which it is the inheritor. Since no poem can be read in the same way twice – each reading is an original encounter – every poem has the potential to disrupt predetermined matrices of identity through the uniqueness of that moment of *voicing*, something made all the more apparent

10 Katherine Schaap Williams, *Unfixable Forms: Disability, Performance, and the Early Modern English Theater* (Ithaca: Cornell University Press, 2021), p. 190.

in recent initiatives involving performance poetry, such as the 'Seen but Seldom Heard' project.[11] In this sense, the 'theatrical prosthetics' which Williams evokes function as the visible markers of the narrative frameworks which attempt to fix the wondrous or unfamiliar body within a delimited range of pre-defined socially-prescribed meanings. In their book *Narrative Prosthesis: Disability and the Dependencies of Discourse*, David T. Mitchell and Sharon L. Snyder explore the multifaceted uses of what they term 'Narrative Prosthesis' as a form of 'compensation' propelled by a 'need to restore a disabled body to some semblance of an originary wholeness'. Literature, art and the media have, they argue, deployed disability as 'a device of artistic innovation', metaphorising deviations from physical norms as tools of characterisation which have often 'entrenched disability's associations with corruption'. In doing so, 'literary efforts to illuminate the dark recesses of disability produce a form of discursive subjugation' which 'leave[s] the disabled body as a troubled and troubling position within the culture'.[12] The unspoken premise underlying the imposition of the prosthetic literary or narrative device is that of *lack*, of a deficiency which is foregrounded even as the promise of restoration, addition, compensation is being touted as the cultural reward of the artist's genius.

I had only an instinctive sense that I did not want, in *Bleed and See* as a whole work, to turn my brother's experiences into a series of metaphors or moral exempla for aspects of the broader human condition, or to polish to a comforting sheen the rough and splintered realities of his fraught embodiment. I did not simply want to 'narrativise' him, but wanted to show *him* beneath the cultures of seeing through which society defined him. In her article, 'The (Narrative) Prosthesis Re-Fitted: Finding New Support

---

11 Caroline E.M. Hodges, Lee-Ann Fenge and Wendy Cutts, 'Challenging perceptions of disability through performance poetry methods: the *Seen but Seldom Heard* project', *Disability & Society*, Vol. 29, No. 7 (2014), pp. 1090-1103.

12 David T. Mitchell and Sharon L. Snyder, *Narrative Prosthesis: Disability and the Dependencies of Discourse* (Ann Arbor: University of Michigan Press, 2000), pp. 5-9.

for Embodied and Imagined Differences in Contemporary Art', Amanda Cachia challenges contemporary artists' willingness to seize on 'a metaphorical opportunity' to use disability 'as a means to convey troubled emotional states', particularly where 'tropes like the obscene, abject, traumatic, or the freak of nature' are mobilised while 'rarely mentioning the connection… to disabled embodiment and affect'. Calling for a new 'critical disability discourse', Cachia urges a moving 'beyond binaries of normal/abnormal and the well-known lineage of "freak" or "enfreaked" representation in canonical art history and popular culture, to explore why certain types of "affect" are represented in forms considered marginal, troubled, and traumatized but also have aesthetic and stereotypical associations with disability without mention'. The burden here, as I understand it, involves a responsibility to utter the unspeakable and seldom spoken of, the emotive root which ligates trauma to the representation of the non-normative body for the *experiencer* of that body. To action this Cachia urges not a rejection of 'narrative prosthesis' as such, but a 'prosthesis [which] can become a more complex embodiment in the hands of both non-disabled and disabled artists'.[13] This articulates, better than I could have, the ways in which the impact of the histories of the abject, 'freakish', and 'monstrous' on those with disfigurements and disabilities can only be understood in and through the body, and in and through the complex and authentic – rather than the idealised or metaphorically mobilised – emotional responses of the individuals who *live* that body.

Whether or not I have gone anywhere near to achieving that aim in *Bleed and See* is not for me to say. What I grasped, then more instinctively and experientially, as opposed to intellectually, was that any 'narrative prosthesis' is not demanded or deployed by those to whose non-normative bodies it is applied, but is often intended to buttress cultural fantasies of the 'perfect' body. I echo Cachia here in endorsing the 'opportunity to reconsider notions of beauty, perfection, and ideal human form so characteristic of classical Greek sculpture and Kant's aesthetics. What beauty can be found in the

13 Amanda Cachia, 'The (Narrative) Prosthesis Re-Fitted: Finding New Support for Embodied and Imagined Differences in Contemporary Art', *Journal of Literary and Cultural Disability Studies*, Vol. 9, No. 3 (2015), pp. 247-49.

human form without the narrative support of the prosthesis?'[14] This is a question with which I grappled in the poem 'The Academic':

> …the Greek statue,
> flaunting its amputations, stood
> brothered to other alien arcana:
> lopped acanthus, ancient
>
> decapitations, the dark circuitry
> of reassembled urns…
>
> In its wet bubble of radiance,
> it was not an idol, but fooled so
> for flesh that a mere touch
> could almost melt the alabaster,
>
> warp the academic's dream. ('The Academic')

And what was the Academic dreaming? The Academic was reaching back across the imperfections of stone, its amputations, its deformities, its mutilations, to an imagined physical perfection. Here, at least, it becomes clear how that dream of beauty depends on the prosthetics of a fantasised completion. The 'body' before the Academic – its own unique beauty – is not what is being *seen*. The prostheses are ours as a culture, our crutches, our means of propping ourselves up when faced with the disorienting, balance-unsettling sight of the non-normative, the extraordinary body. The first part of *Bleed and See* showcases, in many of its poems, a gallery of images and narratives which western society has created – through art, literature, ritual, myth, and even science – to understand, quantify, control, 'fix' or mobilise for ideological purposes, the disfigured, disabled or 'deviant' body. Expressed not through my own 'voice' but through the voices, experiences or prejudices of imagined 'characters', or through meditations on the transmutation of unfamiliar bodies and behaviours into socially-organising nightmares, these poems stage

14 Cachia, 'The (Narrative) Prosthesis Re-Fitted…', p. 262.

the interjecting frameworks which all-too-often dehumanised my brother in others' stares.

In Part 2 of the collection, 'The Boiler House Gallery', I tried to grapple with something which I realised, even then, was much harder to represent, something for which my academic training and reading could not prepare me: my brother as he was, or rather could be in particular moments, beneath these oppressively totalising narratives. In short, I wanted to honour the authenticity and wholeness of his complex emotional world by speaking directly to him and, by drawing on his experiences as well as the self-made myths and images he created in his artworks, allow him to speak back through every poem's act of *voicing*, even if sometimes that process was unsettling or disturbing.

'honest bone': Voicing the Unspeakable

Not long after the diagnosing of George's neurological illness it became apparent that he was losing his ability to speak. Within a few short years he would lose his voice completely. The prospect of not hearing my brother's words, and his not being able to confide in me as he always had when dealing with his disfigurement, and which he would need to do all the more given his advancing disabilities, was particularly terrifying. I found myself engaged in a kind of desperate mission to preserve what I could of his voice, his emotions, his artistic vision, his expansive imagination, his fire, his *presence*, before the most distinctive expressions of these qualities vanished.

The poems in *Bleed and See* became a way of doing this, particularly those in 'The Boiler House Gallery' section. I can see now that the first part of the collection, 'Alien Arcana', was an effort to put into practice what Michael Davidson described in his *Concerto for the Left Hand: Disability and the Defamiliar Body*: 'works of art defamiliarize routinized patterns of thought and usage to speak of the ways that disability challenges ingrained attitudes about embodiment'.[15] More specifically, my interest in the historical materialities of body-image engaged with a profound question: 'What would it mean for the humanities to think through the body and reimagine curricula not around the "history of ideas" but through an armless Venus de Milo, a crippled Oedipus…?'[16] The statues, non-normative subjects of paintings, mummified corpses, human relics, mythical figures, participants of ritual practice and othered bodies which filled the 'Alien Arcana' section engaged with such reimagining, but how was I to confront my brother's own *presence* directly? I also realised that George was himself an artist and that this was a huge part of who he was, how he saw himself,

15 Michael Davidson, *Concerto for the Left Hand: Disability and the Defamiliar Body* (Ann Arbor: University of Michigan Press, 2008), p. xvi.
16 Davidson, *Concerto for the Left Hand*, p. 4.

his identity. I felt I could not properly honour him without somehow capturing his passion for his art. 'Despite the recognition of disability as embedded in social attitudes,' writes Davidson, 'reception of disability in the arts has never been easy, despite the presence of blind, deaf, or disabled figures (Homer, Milton, Beethoven, Kahlo) as signifiers for artistic genius. Even when a critic approaches a disabled artist with sympathy, there is often the anxiety that such art must, at some level, be a form of advocacy rather than a productive element of innovation.'[17] Apply this to poetry and you have the problem in a nutshell. Should I be writing about what was unique to my brother and his vision or should I be performing a 'form of advocacy', one which centred on narratives of resilience, endurance and overcoming? I can see now how the lack of a clearly-sustained moralised narrative was part of the reason for my reluctance to publish these poems. Davidson presents the case in this way:

> A good deal of self-help literature has been written to explain how to "endure" or "triumph over" such adversity, and figures who do – Helen Keller, Christopher Reeve, Steven Hawking – are celebrated as exemplars. This ideology of ableism... helps to reinforce a Manichaean binary that divides the world into lives worth living and those that are not... A critical disability aesthetics defamiliarizes such entrenched binaries to offer not simply a more humanized perspective on suffering but a way of translating the materiality of the artwork, both as form and practice, into the materiality of the different body.[18]

The limits of a 'disability aesthetics' geared solely towards a kind of moral validation is something I can now recognise in a manner I perhaps could not when I originally wrote this poetry collection. After all, I did not pen these poems to make a political or ideological point, so much as to process the crisis of my brother's conditions,

17 Davidson, *Concerto for the Left Hand,* p. 6.
18 Davidson, *Concerto for the Left Hand,* p. xvii.

my role as his carer, and to preserve somehow his voice, to save something of what I knew was in the process of being lost. To build on Davidson's analysis, approaching these challenges with sensitivity involves not only translating the artwork into the materiality of the 'different body', but encountering the materiality of the body, one's lived experience *within* it, in a manner which translates it, with unflinching honesty, back into the artwork; the 'honest bone' to which, as I had written in the poem 'Human Skin', we must penetrate. It is within this honesty that achievement can be recognised, acknowledged and valued. But it is a process full of danger and fire, that confers upon the body which is its locus a kind of alienating grace which incarnates any number of potentially shrieking, scratching, violent, uprooting, emancipated, shimmering, terrorising, mystifying and mystical corporealities which unsettle easy alignments with the culture's self-validating monolithic images of the disfigured or disabled subject.

Let me try to explain this. I am reminded of a comment made by the comedian and broadcaster Rosie Jones who, as described in an article by Steve Clarke, 'recalled that the first disabled character she saw on TV was a school girl in BBC TV's pioneering drama, Grange Hill. Rachel, played by Francesca Martinez, had cerebral palsy'. Jones, who also has cerebral palsy, 'hated the fact that one of the storylines involved Rachel being bullied', commenting that "'I have never felt disabled. So it... made me quite angry... Why is she the only person I have to be compared to? ... Why wasn't there an ultra-cool, ultra-funny person exactly like me?" Jones' quip, "'I had a great time at school and I bullied people'", prompted Adam Hills, presenter of the TV show *The Last Leg*, to chime in "'Why are disabled people on TV always portrayed as being nice all the time?... Why aren't there any [disabled] bastards on TV?'". Beneath the levity an important point was being made about the 'rampant stereotyping' of disabled people in the media.[19] It is one made by Margaret Price – in relation to those with a 'mental disability', but which applies equally to any individual with a physical condition

19 Steve Clarke, 'Where have all the disabled people gone?', 11 April 2017, https://rts.org.uk/article/where-have-all-disabled-people-gone.

which means they are living with a non-normative body – who draws attention to the expectation of 'the implicitly rational mind of the "good" disabled person' who must 'adhere to a "cultural demand of cheerfulness," which is particularly insidious'; insidious because it implies 'a direct erasure' not only of the condition, in the case of 'a person with depression', but of the totality and complexity of emotions and responses which arise from the lived reality of embodied experience for anyone with a disfigurement or disability.[20] They should not be idealised or turned into idols. Nor should they be demonised. Returning to Shakespeare's *Richard III*, and the other side of the saint-sinner disability binary, I recall Sonya Freeman Loftis' perceptive observation in her *Shakespeare and Disability Studies*:

> It is possible… to imagine a *Richard III* in which neither disability nor disability discrimination cause villainy. Indeed, Richard's own attitude toward disability does him more harm than the attitudes of the people around him. Like able-bodied and neurotypical people, people with disabilities have agency, and they make choices. It seems clear that Richard chooses to do violence and not that disability or social discrimination cause violence.[21]

Decoupling the non-normative body from its moral freighting is, it seems to me, a vital and ongoing work. I found, when writing *Bleed and See*, that there were no easy solutions to this and that the encounter with the authenticity of my brother's emotions – and my own – was often an uncomfortable one. It is here, in this very discomfort, that we find that 'alienating grace', as I have termed it, which jolts us out of the stereotypes, mainstays and expectations which prevent us from *seeing* the person *not* behind the disfigurement or disability – indeed, many see their disability as inexorably intertwined with their identity, and therefore not simply something to be bypassed, elided

---

20 Margaret Price, 'Defining Mental Disability', in *The Disability Studies Reader*, ed. Lennard J. Davis (London: Taylor & Francis Group, 2016), pp. 336-37.
21 Sonya Freeman Loftis, *Shakespeare and Disability Studies* (Oxford: Oxford University Press, 2021) p. 44.

or rendered invisible – but beneath the ideological frameworks and cultural prosthetics which construct our own distorted vision of that individual.

'The Boiler House Gallery' refers to the space to which my brother would retreat when he needed to be solitary, to think about his art, or to deal with the traumatic physical conditions with which he was living and their mental consequences. He used to store his art materials there too, so it was for him a safe and familiar space which spoke to him of the potential for creativity. But it must, in the earlier years after his diagnosis, particularly in the wake of his failing eyesight (which was one of his first symptoms), have resonated with the impending loss of that creativity. I imagine that some of the mythologies which he himself created – and which I tried to record in Part 2 of this collection – as ways of processing his experiences and fears, were conceived in the 'Boiler House' in the garden of our parental home. One recurring motif in my brother's artwork was that of the 'mask'. In a way, so many of the figures in the first part of the collection are masks my brother wore unwillingly or which society imposed upon him, reflecting cultural fantasies or forms of talismanic and protective communal mythmaking with which societies and authoritative institutions have historically shored themselves up in opposition to the imagined encroaching, swallowing horrors which threaten order, sanity, physical integrity and health. These emerge in more concrete symbols too, as reminders of the idealised faces which are idolised but unattainable except as haunting or uncanny masks, such as the 'grinning trophies' and 'skins of others' with which we dress ourselves, described in the sardonic poem 'The Valley', the fetishised and exploitative 'immaculate' mask of beauty in 'L'Inconnue de la Seine', or the disquieting mask of a painted iron-skinned 'nymph' in 'Fly on the Canvas'. A question had struck me even while writing these poems: can such powerful processes of mythmaking be appropriated by their demonised or in other ways stereotyped subjects or are those with non-normative traits and 'deviant' corporealities always fated to be their victims? In the 'Boiler House Gallery' section, therefore, I explored the masks my brother created to help him deal with his emotions, particularly those generated by others' reactions to his own non-normativity, as in the poem 'The Ring':

When the children
came to gibe at you
and stick pins
in your scalp, gawking

at the awkward way
your limbs twitched,
you carved
your own prehistory;

and it was the mask
you wore when they danced
in a ring around you.
Pitiless rites. Revenge

was your genius
to make them ask
if the mask was worse
than what it covered up.

('The Ring')

I felt uncomfortable with the idea of publishing these poems for so many years because they simmered with anger. My brother's attempts to make sense of people's cruelty, their hostility to his disfigurement, and their curiosity about his disability, as well as his loss of control over his own body, often ended in a frustrated resignation to this emotion. In the poem 'The Window' I tried to capture the intensity of this response: 'When your limbs/revolted, your anger/could unapparel the sky, burn/a hole in the heart of starlight.' I found it particularly difficult processing my own reactions to the sometimes unexpected and disturbing brutality of the language of poems which were meant as expressions of my brother's own mythmaking in his art. I can see the purpose of this was to do violence to *concepts* of beauty – to the normative and 'superior' body as idea – but it was difficult both to reconcile this with the more tender and delicate collection I often felt I *should* have written and to walk away from the reality of the emotional trauma my brother was experiencing, a trauma accumulated from years of bullying abuse and inquisitive or hostile stares. An example of this reactionary, lashing fury can be seen in the poem 'Dead Reckoning':

> They feared you once, no longer,
> when the devil in your look
> was a magnetic storm that pulled
>
> the air from their lungs, smashed
> the vanity from their pretty faces,
> stripping beauty from the bone.
> My Merrick. Love. I won't forget.
>
> ('Dead Reckoning')

Here I acknowledge my brother's *complex sympathy* for, or rather with, John Merrick, dubbed 'the Elephant Man', one of a range of alienated or 'enfreaked' personalities who were the subjects of his artworks, including cult-figures in the media who are stand-ins for violent and destructive forces, like those alluded to in 'those Hell-Raiser/faces, those Krueger masks' in the poem 'The Boiler House', and the 'freak' clown with 'shark-teeth' in the poem 'Walker' (referring to the popular protagonists of horror films such as *Hellraiser*, the *Nightmare On Elm Street* franchise and Stephen King's *It*). For my brother this complex sympathy meant encountering those faces and bodies *of wonder* in a manner which collapsed the tyrannous binaries of pitiable/good victim and wicked/monstrous assailant: painting or drawing these figures was, for him, a way of making those most-looked-at faces and bodies stare back unnervingly at the viewer. Indeed, in one particularly striking drawing, Freddy Krueger (the severely disfigured protagonist of the *Nightmare on Elm Street* films), glares mischievously at the viewer as if in possession of occult knowledge, a finger to his lips demanding silence. One of his eye-sockets is anatomised, almost fully exposing a menacingly prominent eyeball. His other hand, gloved and blade-tipped, holds a large camera lens which he thrusts forwards, an expressionless inquisitive eye trained on his lookers: Krueger turning the lens back onto the *horrified* consumers and interpreters of his lacerated skin. This, and numerous artworks which engaged with othered bodies in film, was a shorthand instantaneous way of doing what Grace McCarthy describes in her book, *Shakespearean Drama, Disability, and the Filmic Stare*, in which she recommends applying a 'film studies paradigm' to the 'nuanced and complex representation' of the non-normative body, when the filmic stare is 'designed to elicit shock and/or body horror'; a process which is, she asserts, a 'critically valuable' means of engaging with 'disability aesthetics'.[22] Capturing these disturbing portraits in poetry, as reflections not only of my brother's artistic expression but of the self-declarative nature of his own explosive emotional drives, was not easy, but now I can see that it was necessary. It was a way of not forgetting, of preserving my brother's voice, his vision, and honouring – without diminishing or smoothing away – his suffering as well as his strength, while acknowledging his sensitivity to the culture's skewed images of unfamiliar bodies.

Tom Shakespeare, in his article 'Cultural Representation of Disabled People: Dustbins of Disavowal?', stresses the importance of engaging critically with the 'imagery' of 'impairment' within a culture which all too often lacks an analytical vocabulary for the social and aesthetic mechanisms in operation when 'disability… is the most active and prominent metaphor of all, and disabled people become ciphers for those feelings, processes or characteristics with which non-disabled society cannot deal. As a result, those negative aspects become cemented to disabled people'. This 'objectification of people with impairment', Shakespeare argues, is a form of 'fetishism', citing the 'Elephant Man' in relation to 'the freak-show [which] is a clear example of the way that human beings were seen as non-human, as potential exhibits in what was perhaps a cross between a zoo and

22 Grace McCarthy, *Shakespearean Drama, Disability, and the Filmic Stare* (London and New York: Routledge, 2021), p. 6.

a museum'. Drawing on Marx's definition of 'fetishism to refer to the way that social relationships are regarded as things (or reified)', Shakespeare reveals the way in which this results in an interpretation of 'Disabled people… as passive and incapable'.[23] Acted upon, made pliable, rendered inactive, the deviant or non-normative body is *enthinged*, puppet-mastered or back-engineered into its constituent removable – and often interpreted as malfunctioning – parts.

This fetishism is something I am aware there was a danger of reproducing in *Bleed and See*, with its engagements with such histories of objectification. But even while composing these poems I did have an instinctive sense of how this was to be avoided. In her article, 'Body Politics and Disability: Negotiating Subjectivity and Embodiment in Disability Poetry', Katerina Tsiokou stresses the need for a 'departure from traditional, psychoanalytical notions of subjectivity towards more productive perceptions of the subject, as constantly re-defined by interactions with its environment'. She sees this as 'particularly relevant to the experience of subjectivity through disability', providing a 'theoretical framework for justifying and defending corporeal as well as perceptional difference'. An acknowledgement in poetry of the 'transformative potential' of the body, writes Tsiokou, 'as constantly changing and fluid, challenges the conception that the body can be thoroughly studied, deciphered, and controlled', and provides a 'means to resist its normalization and essentialization'.[24] The 'unfixable', deliberately non-harmonious, and liberatingly vacillating nature of the non-normative body is a recurring theme in this critical introduction. One might see here a blending of two critical models which are often defined as separate strands of enquiry, summed up neatly by Grace McCarthy: the 'social model of disability', which 'locates disability as a relationship between an individual with an impairment and a society whose architecture, customs, and assumptions are ablesist… and need

---

23 Tom Shakespeare, 'Cultural Representation of Disabled People: Dustbins of Disavowal?', *Disability & Society*, Vol. 9, No. 3 (1994), pp. 283-299; pp. 286-88.

24 Katerina Tsiokou, 'Body Politics and Disability: Negotiating Subjectivity and Embodiment in Disability Poetry', *Journal of Literary and Cultural Disability Studies*, Vol. 11, No. 2 (2017), pp. 205-22; pp. 206, 214-15.

to change to accommodate more variations of the human body and mind', and the 'cultural model', which presents disability as a locus of identity, 'a site of cultural resistance to socially constructed conceptions of normality'.[25] I can see now, with such critical frameworks in my grasp, that the poems in this collection were attempts at preventing my brother from becoming an object, or a figure simply refracted or fragmented through a series of artefacts and monoliths. Realising this aim meant not presenting him as static or passive, but as metamorphic, endlessly reactive, ceaselessly creative, constantly refiguring the environments and cultures of seeing which sought to pin him down, to *enthing* him. This was a continuation of my brother's own project: his artwork became a *responsive* way of asserting ownership of his own body and I tried to capture that using a visual vocabulary he himself used.

In this metamorphic potential there is something of what Genevieve Love, in her book *Early Modern Theatre and the Figure of Disability*, sees as the 'productive possibilities of disability as metaphor', through which the 'role of the disabled body' comes to embody a 'relationship to transit, to complex movements between media'. The signifying power of metaphor is thus reclaimed through a *performing* body which mobilises diffuse and niftily adaptable 'theatrical energies' as it moves through scenes, settings, and contexts in a manner which is 'anticipated in early modern paratexts'.[26] Similarly, this collection stages the potent resourcefulness expressed through the movement of my brother's body through media – across paint, graphite, word, ritual practice and filmic arts – amplified by its own paratexts and intersecting cultural artefacts (in this regard, this volume's many epigraphs are vital elements of its poems' layered meanings, reflecting their critical engagement with cultural representations of the othered body across media and historical periods). This sense of radical expansion, across multi-modal states,

25 McCarthy, *Shakespearean Drama, Disability, and the Filmic Stare,* p. 3. For further succinct definitions of the differing models of enquiry within disability studies see also Hobgood and Wood, *Recovering Disability in Early Modern England,* pp. 4-6.

26 Genevieve Love, *Early Modern Theatre and the Figure of Disability* (London: Arden, 2019), pp. 4 and 26.

is not undermined or contradicted but paradoxically augmented by an inherent tension within these poems. It was in my brother's own art that the motif of the ritually sacrificed, wounded, and buried body recurred. What pushes against this hemmed-in, claustrophobic, and interred corporeality is the mystical nature of many of these bodies, their abiding, patient, and thrumming anticipation of looked-to moments of transition, from 'Holbein's tomb-laid Christ' in the poem 'The Boiler House', to the 'harvest' of the 'cutters' which turns 'blood/in the loam' into the 'beautiful glimmering of Buddha' in the poem '51', with its allusions to the sacrificial strains of Psalm 51, the very psalm which those condemned to die in the early modern period traditionally recited before their executions. These 'Boiler House Gallery' poems *speak back* to those in the 'Alien Arcana' section which centre on these themes – particularly those which present the feared, abject or wondered-at body as a scapegoat sacrificed for the cleansing of society's ills and deepest anxieties or as a locus of rebirth, including 'Witch Crafts', 'Corn-Mother', 'Totem-Girl' and 'The Secrets of Trees', among others – but do so as acts of appropriation which refuse the stasis of the body as alone an icon of pain, of buried silence, of terminal sacrifice, as with the poem 'Anything But You…':

> …My eyes
> are hostages to this sacrifice.
> Is this what they call a ransom,
>
> an offering? But you out-stare
> my theology, my theoria, god of blades
> and hammerblasts, the scourge
> of the prettyskins, an accidental
> wreaker.
>
> ('Anything But You…')

These violent energies are also the productive pandemonium of creativity, anticipating resurrection and renewal, not through a promised end to, but through the embracing of, a ceaseless change and becoming which resists ideals of beauty and physical perfection.

They also reflect something of the complexity of a poetics of the non-normative body. This collection does not focus on physical disability alone, but on other forms of 'deviant' physicality which generate wounds, scars, and bleeding; corporeal tokens which themselves signify, which speak. In an arresting essay entitled 'Scars in Disability Culture Poetry: Towards Connection', Petra Kuppers deploys 'the embodied sign of the scar to trace ambivalences, shifting meaning and the transformation of personal material into poetic labor'. Scars and wounds, she writes, 'are everywhere, full and empty, sad and sexy, but always a little other, a little beyond and too much to bear'. *Bleed and See* is a collection scratched, scorched, scored, and cut through with wounds and their scar-relics, and it is perhaps this, more than anything, which made it, even for its creator, 'too much to bear'. To return to a theme already encountered, Kuppers states that 'scars as embodied performances' can facilitate '[c]hanging body image, sub-cultural identification, the reclaiming of agency in post-medical encounters'. This helps me make sense of the urgency of those scars in the context of my brother's – and our whole family's – 'post-medical encounters' following his diagnosis. Bleeding again, bleeding anew, is a way of reshaping the meaning of the body. I can see this now, with the aid of my critical enquiries into a poetics of disability, as something my brother needed to do and which the poems sought to reflect. While I find it much harder to see this process – as Kuppers more optimistically does – as 'a move outwards... [c]onnecting across bodies, worlds and pain' to cultivate a kind of universalising poetics of common bodily experience, I can see how it can fashion a 'poetry that can... honor the best we have: our bodies, changing, in time and in connection', with each metamorphosis a unique act, a new performance. My poems were an attempt to take the mythologies of my brother's imagination and 'embody and make available to discourse the knitting together of meaning out of breath, flesh and language'.[27] I have found that so much 'poetic labor' inheres in reading the braille of the flesh, the distinctive and matchless pattern that it creates for each person, as

27 Petra Kuppers, 'Scars in Disability Culture Poetry: Towards Connection', *Disability & Society,* Vol. 23, No. 2 (2008), pp. 141-50; pp. 141-42.

individual as a fingerprint. The poems 'Lip-Reader' and 'Pressure Sore', like others in the collection, call for this kind of precise 'reading' of my brother's pain as he himself navigated his emotions between the lines of art and flesh:

...Lines

of dye and graphite spoke, art hatched through with hurt...

A fresh scar or a tooth-print, any small protrusion,
would have set the record straight, would have proved braille
to our oblivious fingers.
('Lip-Reader')

...We knew
this sham slip would never be the same as you.
It wasn't real DNA that pulsed codes
into your blood but the thick acrylic you'd used

in your works, the shining graphite that caked
each sketch you'd plied...

We knew, as sure as day follows day and wound
follows wound, you would turn, haled whole
through a living canvas-skin, into one of your paintings.
('Pressure Sore')

This is not to say that what is contained in this volume can't speak to others' experiences. Of course it can. Its very structure presents the historicity which contributed to my brother's individual experience, and these are histories we all share. It is simply that they are *activated* differently in each of us, and therefore I resisted allowing the collection to 'land' on a universalising of disability and non-normative corporeality because the point for me was to capture the singularity of my brother's experience, and my own (as brother and carer). This is, in fact, to insist on the uniqueness of everyone's experience, and to celebrate that; as I indicated in the poem 'On Gratitude', which addressed my brother with a reflection on 'the success you made of your life because you made it//your way, even while your body betrayed you at every turn'. I have therefore come to see a virtue in what I had always so feared: what I viewed as the sometimes disturbing and unpalatable nature of the poems in this collection.

The work of poet and critic Emilia Nielsen has given me some additional insights into my own reactions. In her article, 'Chronically Ill, Critically Crip?: Poetry, Poetics and Dissonant Disabilities', she explores the ways in which 'crip theory' – a theorising of disability through the potentially jolting reclamation of the term 'crip' – enables a 'querying [of] what the poetry and poetics of disability might offer, as a mode of writing, theorizing and community making, for those of us who identify as chronically ill'. My brother's illness was classed as 'chronic' long before it was seen as 'terminal'. The way in which these two forms of diagnosis interface with a 'crip' poetics is complex and defies easy explanation. Nielsen provides a framework which breaks down categories in this 'desire to jolt people', to 'shake things up', allowing us to 'query commonplace understandings'. Embracing what she terms 'dissonant disabilities', she advocates a form of poetics which revels in the making of an 'unpleasant noise', which is 'pleasing in its incongruousness and discordant sensibility'. Here I see an echo of something fundamental to my poetry: it isn't always attractive. A 'crip-sensitive poetics' taps into what Nielsen sees as a 'collective responsibility to refuse compulsory able-bodiedness', necessary because 'biomedical definitions of chronic illness do not adequately give voice to the intensity of living with an unrelenting state of bodily uncertainty, nor how this affects identity formation'.[28]

I find here precisely the key to the paradox of collective and individual responses to non-normative corporeality which this introduction has been tracing: so much of my brother's art and my poetry was a response to our coming to terms with the 'uncertainty' of his body's story. The narratives and myths society creates around and

28 Emilia Nielsen, 'Chronically Ill, Critically Crip?: Poetry, Poetics and Dissonant Disabilities', *Disability Studies Quarterly*, Vol. 36, No. 4 (2016).

through the different or extraordinary body are a means of colonising the resonant, the potentially signifying, endlessly reconstitutable void which is this whirlpool of uncertainty. Uncertainty provides an opportunity to turn absences into ideologies, into political statements, into endorsements for an institution's authoritative knowledge, into hierarchies of race, sexuality, gender, physical ability, neuro-normality or simply into ready cash. Here is competition, here is the race, here the struggle, the 'the odds of flesh and fang,/ which meet in the fabric' ('Inhuman Histories'). Indeed, many of the critics and poets we have encountered in this introduction acknowledge that figurations of disability cannot be divorced with any ease from the aggressive masculinity of the colonial project – the way in which curiosity culture is a symptom of the rapacity and possessiveness which attends the othering of peoples from colonised lands, and which is justified through the cultivation of discourses of the exotic, alien or monstrous – or from misogyny and homophobia because, as Tom Shakespeare asserts, the oppression of those with disabilities or non-normative bodies can be 'identified' with a type of colonially-inflected gender stereotyping which 'is the real focus of concerns with potency, with supremacy, and with domination'.[29] Echoing Tsiokou's sense of the non-normative body's responsiveness to the environments it encounters as a vital form of poetic expression, Ally Day, in her article 'Chronic Poetics, Chronic Illness: Reading Tory Dent's HIV Poetry through Disability Poetics and Feminist Bioethics', incorporates feminist studies as a means of disturbing dominant bio-medical narratives through the embracing of uncertainty's potential, which she calls 'unknowing', 'to caution narrative medicine's insistence on knowing and instead propose a practice of feminist bioethics that reads poetry to uncover spaces of unknowing'. This involves recognising the ways in which 'disability poetics, chronic poetics, and feminist bioethics can provide rugged

29 Shakespeare, 'Cultural Representation of Disabled People: Dustbins of Disavowal?', p. 298. See also Nielsen, 'Chronically Ill, Critically Crip?: Poetry, Poetics and Dissonant Disabilities', for the intersections between disability, 'crip' poetics, gender and sexuality. Petra Kuppers offers a concentrated approach to the blending of feminist poetics and disability studies in 'Poetry-ing: Feminist Disability Aesthetics and Poetry Communities', *English Language Notes*, Vol. 49, No. 2 (2011), pp. 73-82.

trail maps through this space of unknowing; maps that may need to be adjusted or rerouted depending on bodily dis/ability and an ever-changing environment'.[30] What are these environments if not spaces of contention and challenge, spaces of colonial conquest and post-colonial resistance?[31]

Many of the poems in this collection present the subtle intersections between figurations of disfigurement and disability and those dark stratagems of the culture which turn corporeal liminalities and uncertainties into the markers of racial, sexual and gendered difference – a *knowing* difference in the sense that these processes attempt to map, define and fix the non-normative body in relation to a range of social certainties, aesthetic ideals or confidently explicated *bodies* of knowledge. These poems are, therefore, attempts to demonstrate how processes which worked to embed culturally those corporeal 'norms' which have become attached to polarising concepts of ethnicity, femininity and masculinity were the same as those which led to the vilifying of 'deviant' bodies (examples of poems engaging with such intersections include 'Cabinet of Curiosities', 'Totem-Girl', 'The Secrets of Trees', 'Vocations', 'Fly on the Canvas', 'The Critic' and others). My sense of responsibility lay with voicing what George had in fact always been speaking, in the creative spaces afforded by these gaping uncertainties: that the exploited or suppressed subject can stake a claim for their own authentic myth-making, can fill those echoing voids with their own

---

30 Ally Day, 'Chronic Poetics, Chronic Illness: Reading Tory Dent's HIV Poetry through Disability Poetics and Feminist Bioethics', *Journal of Literary and Cultural Disability Studies*, Vol. 11, No. 1 (2017), pp. 83-98; p. 92.

31 See Petra Kuppers' 'Trans-Ing Disability Poetry at the Confluence', *Transgender Studies Quarterly*, Vol. 1, No. 4 (2014), pp. 605-13, in which she explores 'a poetics of trans-ing, at the confluence of disability culture and trans cultural expression, indigenous naming of the land and performance trance', exploring the complexities behind a 'movement politics of "trans"—transitioning, transforming, trans-oceanic journeys, states of fluidity' which 'tries to chart its way on foreign terrain with respect and with appropriate uncertainty'. Indeed, Valerie Traub's 'The Nature of Norms in Early Modern England: Anatomy, Cartography, *King Lear*', demonstrates that the technologies for the geographical mapping of land and the earliest developments in the science of anatomy were closely aligned. Jonathan Sawday, in his *The Body Emblazoned: Dissection and the Human Body in Renaissance Culture* (London and New York: Routledge, 1995), also demonstrates the way in which discourses of 'colonization' informed the 'mapping' of the body's spaces.

voice/s, their own meaning/s. Through his art my brother transmuted uncertainty and unknowing into forms of resistance, interrogation and challenge. That, I can see more clearly now than I could then – or at least I can articulate it with a crisper and more self-conscious vocabulary – was the voice I was racing to capture, to render *seeable*, even as my brother's physical voice was fast deteriorating. That was the agitation, the kinesis, the metamorphic energy I was trying to show in his corporeality's *performance* across the varied creative and trans-modal media represented in this collection. If poetry can speak another's voice, it can also voice another's movement, even when their body is losing its ability to self-propel. The paradox of this is that it is no less an expression of their own autonomy.

I have written here of '*our* coming to terms' with the uncertainty of the 'body's story'. This suggests a complexity to this creative act which is not easily defined. My brother did not write this collection. I did. I did not produce the artworks which inspired it. He did. We were collaborators in this collection… we still are. This reproduces the symbiosis which I experienced as a carer for someone who was losing – indeed within a few years of diagnosis had lost – his bodily autonomy; but not, even within the close interdependency of the caring relationship, his identity. Perhaps the biggest challenge for me, now as much as then, is making sense of this when the critical tools largely fail us. How can the caring role help preserve and serve as a catalyst for the expression of individual identity, even in the face of the catastrophic breakdown of the body's functions? How do we *speak* the relationship which is formed through the touch of the carer? How do we voice a shared wound, a shared bleeding?

'into my hands your labours': Towards a Poetics of Caring

Naturally not everyone with a disability will need dedicated carers, but if I achieve nothing else with *Bleed and See* I would like to make a suggestion which arises from my experience of writing and reflecting on this collection: that there is an urgent need for a more sustained, practice-based, critical framework for a *poetics of caring*. The development of critical discourses around carer-poets' writings, cultivated by carer-poets themselves or by poets and critics engaging creatively or academically with the act – the very touch – of caring, will illuminate both the unique features of the caring role and its relation to the fields of disability studies and 'crip' poetics and culture. It is here that I find a troubling, yawning and signifying lacuna in critical-poetics. This was made more apparent when I tried to make sense of something peculiar: anyone acting as a long-term carer for someone with a disability or chronic or terminal illness will tell you that they experience an uncanny form of embodiment which it is very difficult to explain. I tried to sum it up in the poem 'Another Year', though it is implicit in other poems in the collection too:

                    Seasons passed
and I could no longer distinguish

your limbs from mine, your insomnia
from my carefulness to intercept
the first tremoring of need. Oh Father
is this what incarnation is like:
volition as the unfamiliar aggregate
of densities?

('Another Year')

Caring for my brother often meant I was living a kind of symbiosis, in which I could not tell where his body ended and mine began. I had also observed this in my mother's role as a carer for her son, which was at a level of intensity that went even beyond my own experience. As a mother she was doubly corporeally attached to him (flesh of her flesh, having carried him in pregnancy for nine months, and nurtured and cared for him his whole life) and it is important to acknowledge that no matter how many hours I tended my brother – and I found being a carer a continuous *mode of being* – this was only a fraction of the caregiving work my mother poured into keeping my brother alive. I was watching the evolution of both my own caring role and my mother's, witnessing the way it transmuted volition into a shared concept, movement into transferred kinesis, breathing into a contingent process. There was no easy way to define this – no language to give it heft and matter, though it was a puzzle which both resided in and puzzled the body. It is a different *way of knowing*, a different way of thinking about disability identity in those situations where disability and caring are coterminous states.

At the heart of the care-giving function is – has always been – a fusing, coalescing, incarnational kind of corporealisation, a radical interdependency, or what I would term more accurately *intercorporeality*, which has defied explication on a critical level. I struggled to locate studies which pinned this down in a resonantly helpful way. There is existing literature which emphasises the importance of paying attention to 'the voices of carers' in a formal health-care setting, as one study of mental illness puts it: 'It is essential that carers' views and opinions are embraced by health care service providers and inform decision-making on reforms of physical health care services so that the longevity and quality of life of people with mental illness is improved'.[32] As someone who had been a young carer myself, I could see the importance of my relationship to those health-service providers which helped manage my brother's care and well-being. But defining carers primarily within medicalised settings

32 Brenda Happell, Karen Wilson, Chris Platania-Phung and Robert Stanton, 'Physical health and mental illness: listening to the voice of carers', *Journal of Mental Health*, Vol. 26, No. 2 (2017), pp. 127-33; p. 131.

will not give us a complete understanding. As another study reveals, the perception of carers' roles tends to be polarised:

> The medical literature views carers in two ways. First, carers are identified as a group whose actions influence disease course and recovery of people with chronic health problems... Second, carers are viewed as a group 'at risk' of ill health... The carer's role is associated with wide ranging negative effects on their well-being... Young carers' opinions and experiences are unique, yet largely neglected.

Despite a 'growing consensus that the subjective experience of being a carer is critical in determining health outcomes for both the carer and the recipient of care', there remains a limited attention to the ways in which that 'subjective experience' can be made to speak in a creative context. The findings of this study get close to a solution, concluding that this rich store of knowledge can be 'accessed by the "stories" developed to give meaning to, and organize oneself in relation to others'. This process will 'facilitate the adoption of person-centred interventions and support, which should be grounded within the individuals' own framework of meaning'.[33] Hearing the stories of carers is, I believe, important, for all sorts of reasons, not just in relation to maximising medical support and the health of both carer and cared-for individual, but for more subtle, yet no less significant, reasons, such as the acknowledgement of independent identity, for both parties in the caring relationship, as well as creating opportunities for cultivating a sense of life-affirming purpose. Poetry can provide a means of realising these goals, but studies which attempt to understand this uniquely symbiotic relationship on a deeply critical level, and which develop strategies for using creativity and the arts to enrich the lives of those who experience it, are still few and far-between.

---

33 Helen Bolas, Anna Van Wersch and Darren Flynn, 'The well-being of young people who care for a dependent relative: An interpretative phenomenological analysis', *Psychology and Health,* Vol. 22, No. 7 (2007), pp. 829-50; pp. 830-32 and 846.

One area where the role of the carer seems to draw more attention is in the study of Alzheimer's and Dementia. In his article 'Seeing oneself as a carer in the activity of caring: Attending to the lifeworld of a person with Alzheimer's disease', Peter D. Ashworth suggested a framework in which 'the carer may see that the patient is a self: the subject of a lifeworld'. The 'lifeworld' in this instance is a sense of the totality of the patient's experience through which 'the grounding of personhood can be restored in the carer's perception of someone with dementia'. This is activated when 'the carer attempts to pay attention to the current experience for the experiencer', acknowledging at one and the same moment that which is 'essential to all human experience' and expressive of 'the (possible) uniqueness of *this particular* individual person's experience within the general frame of the lifeworld'.[34] There is in this something of the *performative* power we have already explored in this introduction, the possibilities inherent in a heightened awareness which comes from watching oneself in the 'act' of caring, an awareness which presupposes autonomy, choice and the potential for positive and mutually beneficial change. But what of poetry? How might the benefits of the carer's consciously-nurtured self-experience *as* carer be realised in creative acts? One practical study, which did involve creative writing, again focused on 'dementia care' and concluded that:

> ...using creative writing techniques to... mak[e] sense of events, situations and actions in the work place, to manage the complexity of caring for others and/or using creative writing to illuminate... reflective practice can help practitioners consider what action to take to improve their practice and ultimately, the care that they give... Opening up a space to explore one's own

34 Peter D. Ashworth, 'Seeing oneself as a carer in the activity of caring: Attending to the lifeworld of a person with Alzheimer's disease', *International Journal of Qualitative Studies on Health and Well-being*, Vol. 1, No. 4 (2006), pp. 212-25; p. 223. For a practical application of this more theoretical framework, also involving the concept of the 'lifeworld', see Andy Pulman, Les Todres and Kathleen Galin, 'The Carer's World: An interactive reusable learning object', *Dementia*, Vol. 94, No. 4 (2010), pp. 535-47.

> creativity may in turn help the practitioner to 'know' that people with dementia can be and are creative, at whatever stage of disease progression... [T]here needs to be an implicit understanding that all can be imaginative and that health and social care can benefit from artistic involvement. To be 'dementia friendly', we need to understand that people living with dementia are never 'The Other' or 'The Problem'.[35]

There is much here that can be applied across caring roles; not just in the medical setting or the workplace, but in the home, in the school and other contexts. That which resonates with my experience here is twofold: the intertwined awareness of creativity in both carer and person receiving care which a 'poetics of caring' can foster, and the sense of responsibility to provide a channel, through such creativity, for the voice of the individual who may not be able to speak for themselves as readily as others due to their condition. This latter sense of responsibility in particular may account for the fact that studies of the caring role are more abundant in the field of Dementia care than they appear to be across other arenas of medical and social care. The loss of the voice, memories and familiar behavioural patterns in the individual with Dementia or Alzheimer's pushes to the fore questions of identity, choice and rights with a special urgency. Individual identity is also complicated by the intertwined experience of embodiment in the caring framework; a valid concern that intercorporeality does not result in the effacing of *selfhood* for either actor in this complex relationship. Yet this dilemma was something I too experienced profoundly and which I sought to capture in *Bleed and See*.

There are valuable lessons here, therefore, which can enrich and improve other spheres of caring, and which also operate on more subtle levels in relation to the myriad forms of daily

35 Catherine Bailey, Romi Jones, Sue Tiplady, Isabel Quinn, Jane Wilcockson and Amanda Clarke, 'Creative writing and dementia care: making it real', *International Journal of Older People Nursing*, Vol. 11 (2016), pp. 244–54; pp. 252-53.

empathetic acts of caring which may facilitate social congress, productive routine-making and life-affirming routine-breaking, engagements in professional practice, economic commerce and education for those with physical or neural atypicality. Without diminishing the importance of the health-care contexts, I trace the potential of recognising an analogous movement to that which Grace McCarthy has outlined as having taken place through the recent critical interrogation of the 'medical model of disability', which tended primarily to find the locus of the non-normative *within* the body of the 'disabled' subject, and which has been challenged by more complex socio-cultural and political models.[36] This has been reproduced in 'crip culture' poetry's engagement with disability theory. A move outwards – beyond the medical facility alone – to think about the ways in which the role of society, culture, history, and political discourse function in the formation of the carer's role and identity, and how this might be applied to a critical poetics, would be, it strikes me, equally valuable. *Bleed and See* was, in so many ways, a collaboration between me and my brother which emphasised the fact that the individual with even the most severe progressive or chronic illness can remain, and is, 'creative, at whatever stage of disease progression'. I see this not as neglecting vital medical contexts, but radically expanding a discourse of body-awareness and identity already fruitfully established in disability studies in a manner which is open to the insights of the carer, the creative synergies which can emerge from the caring relationship, and the contributions which both carer and cared-for individual can make to the critical discourses which lend meaning and significance to the outcomes of creative practice and which make these beneficially reproduceable across the culture. In the absence of more dedicated studies on the utility of a poetics of caring and its intersections with the field of critical disability studies in our contemporary society, I turn again to poet and critic Petra Kuppers, as I find her concept of 'biological determinism', in her article 'Performing Determinism: Disability Culture Poetry', useful.

36 McCarthy, *Shakespearean Drama, Disability, and the Filmic Stare,* p. 6.

In a meditation on the role of 'crip' poetics in the assertion of individual identity, she writes:

> Reclaiming the word "cripple" is hard, and best done in the poetic genre. I hope that the frisson of figuring it out, open-ended, nonanswered, adds beauty to the labor of criticism, the fine-tuning of an ear (or eye, or touch) to the outlines of the breathing poem… So I can't embrace biological determinism, nailing it down. I can't avoid it, either, disembodying the poet. But I can perform biological determinism, the living nature of flesh, in writerly practice, the site where language knits meaning. I can show crip culture poetry as a site of these performances, of living life.[37]

This 'living nature of flesh, in writerly practice' reverberates with my own poetry, even though Kuppers is not dealing with the carer's role specifically. Flesh and word here are coterminous. I seek and see in this 'biological determinism' a shared creativity rooted in the embodied nature of the carer's symbiotic, intercorporeal, relationship with the often-othered body. This flesh-and-word poetics is therefore a reclamation, a reconstitution of that *othering* in a collaborative challenge to the histories which have imposed it on the non-normative body. But there are still so many unanswered questions: Where do carers stand in disability culture and in a 'crip' poetics? What critical language do we use to understand and explain these complex relationships?[38]

37 Petra Kuppers, 'Performing Determinism: Disability Culture Poetry', *Text and Performance Quarterly*, Vol. 27, No. 2 (2007), pp.89-106; p. 94.

38 One way of answering these questions is to encourage more 'research poetry', which can involve the researcher creating poetry from participants' own written testimonies, interviews and stories, as advocated by Carol Rogers-Shaw in 'Enhancing empathy and understanding of disability by using poetry in research', *Studies in the Education of Adults*, Vol. 53, No. 2 (2021), pp. 184-203. This can, she asserts, 'promote human rights for individuals' by 'drawing on readers' emotional connection to participants', and 'increase accessibility to research with marginalised populations' by 'comprehend[ing] their lived experience'. I see my own translation and recording of my brother's experiences, artwork, vision and 'voice' in this collection as a form of 'research poetry' which communicates its findings about my own and my brother's 'lived experience', an experience which, though in many ways tragic, was and continues to be creative and hence enables positive outcomes and insights.

There is work to be done here to excavate the voice of the carer-poet in a more critically-aware and rigorous fashion, to offer a lexicon, with shape, weight and mass, which can be touched, cupped, held and passed on from person to person; a gift.

In his article 'Poetry as Gift', Henry Hart explains that 'The idea of poetry as a gift is as ancient as poetry itself', with deep sacral roots, for the 'poet, like a priest, uplifts audiences by facilitating their communion with the mystery of the poet's creation, or of Creation itself'. Articulating that mystery, as we have seen, often means addressing the unspoken and unspeakable. And this must be both a wounding and a healing process. Hart cites Seamus Heany's elegy 'Out of this World', from his collection *District and Circle* in which he refers to "'the mystery'" and "the mystic-//al Body" of Christ in the "thanksgiving" ritual of the Eucharist'. In doing so 'Heaney acknowledges the wounding nature of sacrificial gift-giving. But he also consistently affirms poetry as a gift that promotes healing so that one's psyche and culture can be "whole again beyond confusion."'[39] I tried to get to the heart of this strange – this sacrally mysterious – wounding-healing in numerous poems in *Bleed and See*. From the 'loss' made 'conquest' and 'reclamation' in the poem 'On Gratitude', to the poem 'How can I say', in which I reflect on the act of caring as both a form of mutual wounding and a gifting of devotion, 'when the teeth… beneath your skin,/as I washed/and dressed you,//fed me with/poison I felt for/love'. The sacred and 'remedial' nature of this exchange is one I also sought to capture in the poem 'Rough Medicine':

> So between our souls there is a ribbon of arsenic,
> working
> our prayers' rough medicine into remedial scars.
> Taking
> into my hands your labours, each sweatdrop precious, worth
> stealing,
> like annealed mercury, I let you sting and sting again.
>
> ('Rough Medicine')

39 Henry Hart, 'Poetry as Gift', *The Sewanee Review*, Vol. 122, No. 1 (Winter 2014), pp. 55-74; pp. 55 and 74.

The gift of poetry is much like the gift of caring: I found it moves both ways. My brother's life was a gift to me; with wounding and healing a mutual exchange. It is true that the consistent refrain of this critical introduction has been the validating and valuing of the individual's embodied knowledge and the distinct and distinctive ways in which this is expressed. But ultimately I do believe this *can* lead to the healing of the culture. Not through a universalising, easy or instantaneous recognition of our oneness, but through a necessarily painfully slow process; achieved person by person, and gifted person *to* person. The best gift is that which responds to and celebrates something unique within the individual to whom it is given.

So, to gift this mystery of healing, where do we begin? It must be with experience. Bleed and see…

PART 1: ALIEN ARCANA

...we know the receipt of all the receptacles of blood, how much blood the body can have; so we do of all the other conduits and cisterns of the body; But this infinite hive of honey, this insatiable whirlpool of the covetous mind, no anatomy, no dissection hath discovered to us.

—John Donne, *A sermon preached at Whitehall*, 8 April 1621

Human Skin

After an exhibition of wall-portraits by Vasiliki Gkotsi

He is no more a victim than I.
He is aware of his deformity
and is confronting us with it.
To stop misprision of the face

light clean as bone must cleave
these dyed tissues from
the honest bone beneath.
I arrange them, dried through,

in layers over the canvas,
pressing vellum with wax
to the wall, to effect skin,
or rather, seeing through skin

to the underlife, that glamourside,
that will surprise us. You must
have asked if these are cracks
in brick-work or merely clumps

of scarred tissue; a step back
and the wrack and sable of this face,
in its imperishable contours,
will show he is our instigator.

And we will stand like this (for this
is my intent), in groups sometimes
of two or three, allowing his eyes
to accuse us gently till our horror

no longer visits us in waves
or whispers, till we see ourselves
in those whose husbandry we do
not own. Learned connoisseurs,

(for you have come to judge
each peek and grimace of my art),
quantify the way this image
meddles with our certainty of love.

Explain how we have lived outside
the coils of his thick wet hair
and the rude prisms of his nostrils.
Clarify how with them he provokes

in us dreams of what the crucible
beneath the skull may be. You have
discovered us with empty hands,
and no mad toil for a motive.

The Academic

> [A]t first sight sculpture, with its solidity of form, seems a thing more real and full than the faint, abstract world of poetry or painting. Still the fact is the reverse... That white light purged from the angry, bloodlike strains of action and passion, reveals, not what is accidental in man, but the tranquil godship in him, as opposed to the restless accidents of life. The art of sculpture records the first naïve, unperplexed recognition of man by himself... [and] is the highest expression of the indifference which lies beyond all that is relative or partial.
> — Walter Pater, *The Renaissance*, 1873

The academic was dedicated
to this cleft inviting possibilities
with stone, a sea-bone locked
to a stash of coral. Moon-man, earth-

fallen lightstealer, the Greek statue,
flaunting its amputations, stood
brothered to other alien arcana:
lopped acanthus, ancient

decapitations, the dark circuitry
of reassembled urns,
pored over by the daily hordes
of nomadic philhellenes.

In its wet bubble of radiance,
it was not an idol, but fooled so
for flesh that a mere touch
could almost melt the alabaster,

warp the academic's dream.

Inhuman Histories

On a collection of Lincean Natural Historical drawings in Windsor Castle, made with the aid of one of the earliest microscopes gifted to the Lincean Academy by Galileo

He that takes delight to understand the wondrous works of Nature shall taste the true pleasure and content of Histories... although the feebleness and weakeness of many appetites are commonly accustomed to stay at things lesse profitable, which is the desire to know new things, called curiositie.
—Joseph de Acosta, *The Natural and Moral History of the Indies*, 1590

[W]onder is the child of rarity, and if a thing be rare, though in kind it be no way extraordinary, yet it is wondered at.
— Francis Bacon, *Novum Organum*, 1620

As lava forms a continent, so an idea
broke and bled its intent. The earth is gentle,
its palatial eye showed us, a pulsing
jellyfish orbiting an underwater inferno.

The sun is the *omphalos*, cross-starred
with our world and we are rapt;
for there are meeker wonders, shivering,
noiseless, beneath the crust of this.

The tomes record how Galileo's gift
to the Linceans, the lens-box,
little *occhialino*, could lay bare
the cunning common tricks of glass-

walking flies; tell the sudden bliss
of seeds calving into daylight;
plumb the throat of a goose-quill.
On every painted folio the Baroque

discovered its own furtive prototype
in misshapen gourds, citrons cicatrised
in alien skins, tumescent siamese fruit,
shrieking mandrake-roots, rude

humunculi of *orchis italica*,
a four-legged chick, a two-headed rat,
a baby's face on a calabash.
Such prodigious sights! To think,

Nature's cack-handed executioners
have left us this crude opulence
of irregularity. Without it we are trustful
as children, not knowing the lines

of suggestion, the odds of flesh and fang,
which meet in the fabric. To turn the page
is to list forwards. My fingers trace
the crooked inhuman illuminations.

Bartholomew Baby

This was water-life if ever she saw it,
a shell-settled god, the profile misused
with a useless ridge of knuckle, fusing
collarbone to carina. The midwife made
the sign, with *Pater, Ave, protegere*,

low-intoned as if this was all no more
than a rumour; the head no precious
clod of mined ore, the spine no broken
rosary in her hand. The 'unlucky bairn',
curled like a gryllus in a medieval folio,

inhabited the tooled margin of wonder,
and would be, just as she had once seen
on the painted board of a Bartholomew Fair,
'Portent of dire wrack, the hammer of God
in our latter times'. Would they one day lay out

a penny to view this witch's changeling
torn from nature's smooth endearments?
The mother's arms will hold a bag of ash.
When the word-gatherers arrive she will know
the world has come between her and her son.

Excavations

i. The Valley-God

A childless Egyptologist discovers a mummified foetus

His head in my hands
was a ball of balata-sap,
an opulent amber globe,
his eyes two stopped glands.

The Nile-sand had dyed
his once-waxen skeins
a golden boult, no cursor
of the bitumen inside.

What ash, what culm lies
in the emptied organ-beds,
muddled with amulets
in oils calcified to glass,

can only be guessed at.
If a valley-god, long-dead,
can stare from the face
of a foetus, into the heart

of the paradise he has lost,
who will dare snub faith
before this mute necromancer
of touch, the linen ghost

whose weight brings back
the ache that rocked
itself between the worlds
a mother cannot cross?

ii. Scarab-Heart

The British Museum, Egyptian Galleries

With what fatal crop or resin
will we find the corpse packed,
cutting first through its skins
of rotten linen, opening

the bone-altar to the air
and spore-witherings' silent
sacrilege? What will
the diligence of hands turn

over to theft or publicity?
Will we find the scarab-heart
beneath the gauze soaked
in Palestine-bitumen, layers

of Nile-mud and saw-dust,
or a real heart shrunk back
to a black blood clot, useless
as a bat's eye? And could

a physician, like me, careless
of theology and meninges,
have left wedged in the little
conjuring-place of the occipital

foramen, the bronze sculpting-
hook with which he had emptied
this skull of dynasties? Under
the baffling light of the CAT scan,

the head is a jellyfish; coils
of damaged tissue still visible
through its diaphanous hood.
The spine's shivered tentacle

has released its bioluminescent
toxins and made a rorschach
of the crippled body: we all see
exactly what we want to see.

The Cabinet of Curiosities

After the collection of Frederik Ruysch in Amsterdam

> I have arranged a Cabinet, in which I have put many things noteworthy and monstrous, that I have taken from the womb of the earth, which bear certain witness to my teachings, and no man will be found who will not be constrained to own that they are trustworthy, after he shall have seen things that I have prepared in my cabinet.
> — Bernard Palissy, *Discours Admirables*, 1580, trans Henry Morley, 1855

> [I]t being lawfull to enter the very bowels (as I may say) of her secresies, not without infinite pleasure I penetrated her *Arcana*, and opening her *Cabinet*… [I found] her full of *Curiosities*.
> — Robert Basset, *Curiosities: or The Cabinet of Nature*, 1637

It was with one outrageous flourish
that they were hauled into the candle-light;
the cleave of plume and incisor behind glass,
a pickled baby's hand, a baby crocodile.
Opening the cabinet I saw in the flesh
what I had only seen before in compendia:
the *Indonesian Natural History*, the bound

scribblings of the *Dutch East India Company*.
There were peaked specimens pinned upon
velvet-covered trays, myriads of butterflies frozen
in parodies of flight, like little fireworks,
and other wonders: mechanical boys,
tulip-bulbs, wax-injected anatomies, and
Jamaican drinking-cocoa, all neatly labelled.

The collector has excelled himself and we have
rarely been this civilised. And is it after all absurd,
to keep creation in a draw, to understand
the simple knot of shard and ligament under
a lens, clean as the swing of a pendulum, or
as the ancient hunger. It is not love that moves us
to accumulate. I keep a lock of my dead wife's hair.

Clone

On Lennart Nilsson's embryological photographs, Life *magazine, 30 April 1965*

And the blots of nature's hand
Shall not in their issue stand.
Never mole, harelip, nor scar,
Nor mark prodigious such as are
Despisèd in nativity
Shall upon their children be…
— William Shakespeare, *A Midsummer Night's Dream*, 5.1.400-405

This is art as judgement on history: our future unfolds
not in a clean line from cause to effect, but in small bursts
of radiation, a flower spreading its silky fingers in every direction

all at once. This is a Cyclops' eye locked on its dream of shape.
Globes of oxygen limp and pop from tiny hooks which quiver
into trilling nerve and root for rotted bone. Each pearl of DNA is looped

upon a filament of breath which stretches from birth to the end of fear.
Little cosmonaut, rebel child scorning warnings on plastic bags,
exploring suffocation like a connoisseur, somnambulant waterwalker,

I have so much to tell you I hardly know where to start. Then again,
when you are old enough to know, like me, you'll say less than your first
cry could. These secrets will lie in you like a buried caul, omentum-eater.

My gatherer of hopes and of diseases. Wonderful parasite. Every day
your expressions are a museum I return to for prospects, correcting me.
You bite my fingers. And when you smile your smile bites little Jesuses.

Killing Time

On the emblem of Time and Death, from Francis Quarles'
— Hieroglyphics of the Life of Man, *1638*

Take back the mark on his back,
the brands on his hands, wicked runes,
the profane cuneiform that marked
him for a pupil of the martyrs' school.

Take back every device whose volt
engaged to shock or buckle
the dark obligations of human skin.
They're yours to use again, lay out

upon some other lover, or turn
against yourself, as the tree-sap
tapped from the bark will replicate
a wound to heal itself, working

the scar to a golden torc. Take back
these adornments, keep them
to adore another's crimes, the way
a butterfly adores its own escapology

inside the cocoon. You too, free
of one body can possess the next,
my killing Time, and bonecraft,
even tissues of the memory,

with all their tender slanders,
will be yours to do with as you please.
This is not disease. Your desire
will make equation with loss with ease

and all the tremors, hairpin cracks,
disturbances in cells, harelips, carbuncles
we think we fear, will be your gifts,
each damaged gene an answered prayer

turning from dialect to solid stone.
Then all the saints you've canonised, arranged
in your hunter's gallery, will outface
the bloodfaced self-assurance of the damned.

Dark Time

At the observatory

> And this endless *addition* or *addibility* (if any one like the word better) of Numbers, so apparent to the Mind, is that, I think, which gives us the clearest and most distinct *Idea* of Infinity...
> — John Locke, *An Essay Concerning Human Understanding*, 1689

You've heard of dark matter I take it.
Well, what of dark time? Does it move
with dwarfs and giants, with the red-shift,
the atomic sift, of worlds in the eternal
dormitories of heaven? If it does, I'm sure

dark time has little to do with precision,
with what we grasp, wonder-tied, in
the mind's habitual chronometer. It's more
a question of the smallest of reparations,
stemming the bleeding asymmetries of space.

Imagine the stars are scars congealed
over this leprous layering of skin upon skin
we call the linear. In time dark time will cut
its healing shapes, covering each breach
where light and life peep through. Picture,

if you can, the floating cells of dark time;
they are continents, colossal islands, coasting
with millennial drifts, or dancers turning
to the measure of their reach, for whom
each arc they make defines a great beyond.

The time will come when we with them will cross
our shuttered thoughts, when memory merely
leans on the body. Then what we think of as dark
will be no more than the captivity of love,
in serving time to spur the dream of freedom.

Witch Crafts

> [T]o afflict the Witch, causing the evil to return back upon them... stop the urine of the Patient, close up in a bottle, and put into it three nails, pins or needles, with a little white salt, keeping the urine always warm: if you let it remain long in the bottle, it will endanger the witch's life: for I have found by experience that they will be grievously tormented...
> — Joseph Blagrave, *The Astrological Practice of Physick*, 1671

i. The Book and the Rope

If the children were possessed
then Satan slept, tired after his tumbling,
when the judgement was passed.

The witch was marked for a feeder of familiars,
a curse-raiser.

Now she would be set to view,
marred by the sift of breath in the clearing
when the townswomen bay for her blood.

The witch has, these last years, kept a home at Amesbury,
with her daughter and her daughter's nurseling
(They say the little one has a fold of skin
at her nape shaped like a monk's cowl).

The house has lain empty since
the inquisitor arrived
bringing toiling instruments, bringing
the book and the rope.

ii. The Witching Charm

Take what pitch the oilbird proffers
down coalface, coarse tarred way,
and you come upon the nude slope
of Stowmarket tor where they say

the twisted bones of two bewitched girls
were raked from the wet loam.
An upturned witch-bottle was buried
between their earth-stopped ears

four hundred years ago, a withered
uterus hardened to saltstone by time,
the inside lined with powdered gold
to which its enchanted unguents had been

reduced in the kiln of their own
human alchemy. And so nail-parings
long-chain fatty acids, hair, urine,
and two perfect silken hearts stabbed

with bent brass pins, exchanged their natures
in the Frechen clay, till the curses
were spent upon the limping daughters
this witching charm could never have saved.

Corn-Mother

> When children wish to go into the fields to pull the blue corn-flowers or the red poppies, they are told not to do so, because the Corn-mother is sitting in the corn and will catch them… [I]t is said that the Corn-mother, in the shape of a female puppet made out of the last sheaf of corn and dressed in white, may be seen at midnight in the corn-fields, which she fertilizes by passing through them; but if she is angry with the farmer, she withers up all his corn… [T]he Corn-mother plays an important part in harvest customs. She is believed to be present in the handful of corn which is left standing last on the field; and with the cutting of this last handful she is caught, or driven away, or killed.
> — Sir James Frazer, *The Golden Bough*, 1922

Corn-Mother, Harvest-Queen,
your slow embodiment was boon
and kenosis for the reapermen
who cut you, dancing, bowelled
and bundled, from the last kirn.

A crossed spar and their scythe-craft
hewed you to an earth-born cult.
Your mouth was a nest of torn flax,
each breast a stamped wheat-cake,
your gravid rush-work becoming

a cage for the tiller's theft and spoil.
They packed your head with loam,
willing seeds and the quick blue
of corn-flowers, and for your eyes
they sewed shining saints' phylacteries.

Then they beat you and ducked you,
beat you and called you witch,
till the two prettiest girls carried you
home in the gathering-dray to be hanged
from the collars of the barn-struts,

dead-watcher of the threshing-floor,
your womb the season's ossuary.
Beautiful scapegoat, your children
do not hate you. They kill you to set
you free. You'll see, when the chaff's

winnowed out, the grain-hoard blessed,
they'll bring you offerings of light. Then
you'll know how many finer skins of love
reveal themselves when the world melts
down to flint and hallucination. Torqued

to your cord of gold, a drop of softened amber,
you'll witness the act of creation winding
itself inward like a blower's abandoned glass.
Collapsing into the phases of victim, omen,
woman of straw, you'll slide from your keel

to your home in the reaplands, where
you'll wait out another incarnation, another
sacrifice, lending your heave to the fable:
when the cob-stalks sway, the Corn-Mother
is dancing among the flaming umbilicals.

Totem-Girl

> Fetishization. This is especially useful in evoking erotic fears or desires and establishing fixed and major difference where difference does not exist or is minimal. Blood, for example, is a pervasive fetish: black blood, white blood, the purity of blood; the purity of female sexuality, the pollution of African blood and sex. Fetishization is a strategy often used to assert the categorical absolutism of civilization and savagery.
> — Toni Morrison, *Playing in the Dark: Whiteness and the Literary Imagination*, 1992

Little Surinam-girl,
little leper. Are these
really your bones,

this miracle of earth,
your harvest of hair,
these tufts, these parings,

the villagers are bearing
away in cupped hands?
Is this what they found,

cutting: your heart
in the puma? Are these
sinews what the vulture ate?

Will the bone-man come?
Will he put you together?
Will the wolf-catcher prise

your ribs from his prey, lift
netherworlds to return them,
piecemeal, to your corpse?

Now the outsiders are here.
They stand around the vessel.
Their modern medicines

are useless, but they are
enjoying the show;
the rattling beads, the rows

of dried rodent carcasses,
a side-scuttler with devices
of trust and coloured

feathers... A pale girl moves
out of the crowd, outweathers
my curiosity. I'm tethered

to her grasp. She takes the tip
of your fingerbits and bites.
Love is a staged digestion.

L'Inconnue de la Seine

In the 1880s a young woman's body was recovered from the Seine. The girl's death-mask, with its impossibly serene smile, captivated Parisian society and became the centre of a cult. The mysterious woman came to be known as 'L'inconnue de la Seine'

As if you had been kissed into death, a smile
so free of need
it demands our faith in hopeless causes,
you remain

immaculate in my conception; mine, every man's,
L'inconnue de la Seine.
They hauled your young body, a white quantity of God,
from the black water,

laid you out in the white ward on the slab
of the Paris morgue.
You were torqued, and had the silver majesty
of a Himalayan burial.

Your stomach was a tooled gourd, like the hollow casks
they hung from the struts
of stonehouses in Carcassonne's Cathar-country:
a snarl of vines

meandering around allegories of greed and lust
figured in a fools' ship
of lapsing priests and gargoyle-eyed cowled monks.
Was that what brought you

here: someone's greed, someone's lust? Were you
a gravidwork
wrung clean of origins before you acquiesced
to the knowledge of depth;

a butchered lag cut-through and dumped,
then plastered over
by a guilty lover; or were we fooled?
Are you just one

of a thousand faces from an assembly-line,
a money-spinner,
modelled on the pretty daughter of a factory-owner
in some squalid verge

of the lower left-bank, a charming sham to grace
a thousand student digs
and half-lit rooms of poets?
When we're done

with elegies what belongs to us?
One harvest of this loss?
Oh no, we've killed you twice
in our rage to possess

not you but our love for the space
behind your mask
which keeps at one remove
the pressed pink cheek and parted lips

we'd stake our dreams on.

The Secrets of Trees

i. Myrrha

After a sixteenth-century Italian birthing dish painted with a scene from Ovid's Metamorphoses, *depicting Myrrha giving birth to Adonis after she had been transformed into a myrrh tree; preserved in the Victoria and Albert Museum, London, England*

Mid-stride she felt the earthpull
of the root-sap at her heel-ball,
her moss-sunk foot hooked
under thorn and bracken-shoot;
sensed the spiralling tendrils seeking
their completion in vein-ducts,

tubers exchanging kisses for blood,
back-pumping resins through. Thrilling
the air her arms slivered into branches,
her fingers' lipped tips releasing
blasts of oxygen. Her skin peeled back
its leaves, festooning foliage, gathering

beneath a fine wood-grain, a feast
for the husk-abiding termites
into which her hair's dark crop
was quickening to drop a seedpod
into her hollow. Just before her brain
dwindled down to its last sop,

a ridged mushroom puffing out
its memories as spores,
she glimpsed her changing body
in the river's honest mirror,

its jutting splintered bones,
bark-weaving scars, all epiphanies

of motion woodlocked into her.
Her yawning mouth became an owl's lair,
teeth popping as kernels lobbed down
into the wastes, her tongue a clod
tasting carbons. As her scream hushed
to a rustle, eyes' buds sprouting, she looked

into her deformity as if it was a gift
and, finding a quavering living thing
inside, she cursed and blessed the disease
that brought her here, to burrow into
the world's odium-stems and origins
of rot, to tarry for the tree-cutter's cure.

ii. Hamadryad

After 'Lady Lazarus' and 'Edge', from Sylvia Plath's Ariel

Cruel mouths bloom crimsons
through my surfaces. Scratching out,
my fingerblades are stained

with bloodberries' burst intoxicants.
Today I am Hamadryad,
bark-trapped, slashed and stashed,

ripening toothed existences.
What man or beast
dare stare this chimera out?

Witch I, the occult-wombed,
a stabbed doll for a rival's parts, the silver
foetus in a jar for conjuring. Beneath

my cracked lids black petals are melting
tears' sears to congeal
into something precious and garish:

Psycho-Queen, supreme lacerator,
bragging my self-adornments
like a professional Narcissa.

My hands are burning.
It is with a queasy yearning that I strive
to see a snake-skin clarity in me,

the hopeful neatness of a saint's deheading,
the soul a gleaming thread
pulled from the wound. Then I shall say

It is done. It is finished.
The martyr is made.
The hero.

This woman.

And I shall love
what I can only half
destroy. My palms are ash.

What glory to unburden the body's story.
All words and all flesh.
I shall shed what I no longer need,

unpeel the scab of this mask and slip through,
a rebirth from a bath of sap and acid,
with most of my lives biting.

Then I will shine.
A white nadir.
Cleaner than death.

Vocations

> Notwithstanding they know these and many such miseries, threats, tortures, will surely come upon them… yet either out of their own weakness, or depraved nature, or love's tyranny, which so furiously rageth, they suffer themselves to be led like an ox to the slaughter;… they go down headlong to their own perdition…, men leaving the natural use of woman…
> — Robert Burton, *The Anatomy of Melancholy*, 1621

i. Woman's Work

The village painter was a peasant like the peeler,
so could turn his hand touchably to her purchase
of the stalk, its sprain and prising hard from the head.
A boy, bare-footed and barely in the frame, watches
her scoop out the eyes, dense jetstone and amethyst,
with small heft and loot, a light labour, the booty
dropped in the bag with the other spoils: bruised
nuggets of muscular tissue, too tender to keep. The boy
is eager to watch, it seems to me, preferring the round thud
of the potatoes in the black bowl, each one scrubbed white
as a lit bulb, to the unhappy chatter of the men outside.
Their faces at the window - a howl behind each mask -
stare blindly after him, fearing ruin in woman's work.

ii. Man's Work

After the painting 'A Fete at Bermondsey' by Georg Hoefnagel, c. 1569-70, Hatfield House, Hertfordshire, England

For me the Bermondsey Feast is the honouring of the faerie queene,
the lucky mooch and breather in the summer progress's long last leg.

Can paint be heard? The snap and lick of the roast-spit; the bare-armed men
in the glow; in the raft of sunhaze, the buzz of airborne lives turning tricks

on stamen; heat tar-thick over head and haulm; wholesome sweat.
This is man's work, laic-work. The faerie queene this way comes. Beyond

the composition, her ladies-in-waiting lift her train. In the frame's endless
here and now, shuck and honeyed flesh depend on the give of a dowel.

The Valley

On discarded schematics for the Olympic village

> Another type of slave is the working-class foreigner who, rather than live in wretched poverty at home, volunteers for slavery in Utopia. Such people are treated with respect, and with almost as much kindness as Utopian citizens, except that they're made to work harder, because they're used to it.
> — Thomas More, *Utopia*, 1516, trans. Paul Turner, 1965

The threads of your smile. Old news.
My familiar or my slow lobotomy? Let not
our halting bodies' slashes shame us!

We'll go all our days *All' Antica*,
take a small boat to the bloodcourse
of the Lea Valley where the locals

claim outmoded gods still cavort
beneath the silver towers
of the sewageworks. Abandoned gods:

they have no place to go. Perhaps
we'll catch them for our train.
We'll have our Ariadnes and our Sybils,

some stopped in airless jars, some
twisted into pitiless machines,
dance for us like celestial marionettes.

We'll make them call down baffled shades
and watch dead tyrants bicker
over palaces of bone.

We'll teach our Olympians to love again,
and for our sport we'll have them turn
the cityscape we've left behind

into a mountain of iron. Here
on the polluted river's bed we'll romp
with dirty Nymphs, while urchins

with peacocks' eyes bite down
on the yellow arteries of flowers,
their jointed limbs our rosaries,

and, royal hunters in the boudoirs
of the Titans, we'll win the pelts
of unspeakably savage things: fat cats,

feral children, the odd stray tourist.
We'll hang grinning trophies
over the silk faces of our prettiest gods

and together we'll see the world
through the skins of others
as one by one the city lights blink out.

Dirt-Apocalypse

> It seems much too big for the largest dolphins, porpoises, or swordfishes, and too little for a true or grown whale, but may be the bone of some big cetaceous animal... We are not ready to believe that wherever such relics of fish or sea animals are found the sea hath had its course...
>
> —Thomas Browne, Letter to William Dugdale, *On a bone dug from a cliff*, October 1660

Midwife to the earth I grubbed for pillage,
and unhusked at last, for want of better saw,
a curious animal. Enfleshed it had been
rigged at the knee and elbow joints, indicating

a life of prayer, the whole form collapsed
in on itself like a wet pot wrecked on the wheel.
It is, I admit, a sect I do not recognise, despite
my expertise. I expect to see some marks

of genus: leathery pouches, cuneiform tablets,
wedges in the ribs as from a lashing-belt, a close-
fitting veil or boater. But we have none of these.
How it got here I cannot tell. We may speculate

some cataclysm has cast it tor-ward or, weighed
in the balance with pure altitude, the riddled hulk
was dropped in a storm, sunken in time to lie here
God knows how long. Has the world grown colder

since it snuck into its blister in the hill; shelled
inland, another Job, another Ezekiel? Is this why
it has this worrying in its look or is it that from
the distance of burial and rot all faiths look the same?

Oracle Bone

A mere wedge of burnt scapula-bone
would have served an oracle of the Shang

dynasty. One such would have sat alone,
with time enough to smoke whole forests

of green tea with silver jasmine, tooling
porous ox relics and tortoise carapace.

With these he could rehearse fortunes
from the clefts in the tortured staves.

Tourists come to see him, shillings
flipped to the organgrinder. Somewhere else

a curtain is drawn back, a fire lit. Painted girls
turn china cups, and turn them again, while here

nerveways and memories are cut back
into the shell that forsook them; his fingers

curled with custom, his eyes unfixed
as flecks of gold leaf in a cold saint's cell.

A Covent Garden Miracle

At present the saints still labour in the work of the flesh, but after the Last Day they will rejoice in symphony and praise. For now the flesh constrains the spirit within the flesh…

— Hildegard of Bingen, *The Book of Life's Merits*, I. 38, trans. Mark Atherton, 2001

His speech was all thrum and coloratura;
to hear it alone would never have betrayed
the standing wreck, the gauze stuck fast to the grain
of his skull-plates, a pelvis like a hangman's tree.

Well then you would have lost a world of wonder.
When his jaw moved, I swear, it worked him up
to a diamond-cutter's shank. With every verse and chapter
the lavish outcrop of his ribs would swell, a lobster poised

around a limpet. This modern Syrinx, with only a crate
in the Covent Garden for a pulpit, sang
of the Second Coming, of kings and beggars
reduced to their escutcheons in the blast, of painted

women losing symmetry in the meltdown,
of priests' mouths turned to clyster-pipes, young men
draining themselves out soft into sudden corpses, history
changing its mind on itself; strange celestial buggery.

I watched him carp his creed. If I ever had a thought
to call him poor bastard, it sloughed from me like a leper's surplus.
His eyes were a puzzle of darkness and freedom. I know this:
I have never seen so much nor known such bliss.

Methods of Darkening

i. The Anatomist

After Rembrandt's Anatomy Lesson of Dr Nicholas Tulp

> [M]an is moved as the Automata, things of motion, Clockes, and the like, engines of wit, that move from a weight without that poseth them: if they doe any good, it is from somewhat without that swayeth their aymes and ends, and not from an inward principle: nature works from an inward principle... artificiall things are forced. Thus good men are distinguished from those that are seemingly holy...
>
> — Richard Sibbes, *A Fountain Sealed: or, The duty of the sealed to the Spirit*, 1637

"You are mistaken. It is but a machine.
Opening the forearm, the keen slide
Of pulley and hinge resists inertia. Pinion
And gavel collude beneath the fleshwork".
A student frantically interrogates his copy
Of Vesalius' *Structure of the Human Body.*
Under the table a scrawny puppy has rolled
Himself indifferently into a ball beside
The slop-bowl. "Observe the twisted
Filaments, metallic spindles, arrogant slivers,
The galvanised edges, the worn gilding.
Touch here, and the arm rises, the whole engine
Inventing space as it extends". The anatomist
Has made a burlesque of his hand.
Another student smiles. There is something
comical in these deathly imitations.

ii. Extreme Solutions

> Then let them anatomize Regan; see what breeds about her heart. Is there any cause in nature that make these hard hearts?
> — William Shakespeare, *King Lear*, 3.6.73-5

We arrive at the point in the anatomy
when the gourd is discovered, and being
opened, must yield itself to judgement.

Those who have meted out from breakfast tables
flesh that forgets the layering of albumen,
how toughened to silk, have come to know -
and to covet - this one natural law:

every kind of shell is lined with skin,
some oily membrane coating the inside,
whose perishability we choose to distrust.

The rest of us, looking on this dearth of life,
may now, with regret of the design, wish no less
for the softer fabric of our existence; our own bones
growing over it like plated armour. What carriage
would then be here, what bearing, totem
of clawed things; hair, blood-channellings,
nipples, turned inward to methods of darkening.

Fly on the Canvas

'Why are you stripping me from myself? Never again, I promise! Playing a pipe is not worth this!' But in spite of his cries the skin was torn off the whole surface of his body: it was all one raw wound… Then from these tears… [flowed] the clearest river in Phrygia, and bears the name of Marsyas.
— Ovid, *Metamorphoses*, Book VI, trans. Mary Innes, 1955

The opportunity was vexed with my own sense of flight
as an act of surgery. I wanted the fly to envy the insolence
of painted flesh, its lack of rapture for depths not its own.
I wanted it to hate the Bacchanals and the glamour of satyrs;
the tyranny of bodies suspended in the bioluminescent globs
of their own perfection. I even spoke to the fly.

Stab it
with some hook or spool for his chicanery,
air-botherer, make a changing scene,
play your invisible violin in mockery.
She will never sing our pain. The painter has betrayed us.

Is there no poison-spit you could feed
with one pulse to warp and mottle
our devices? See how she catches our thoughts,
head turned back, but eyes accusing us
instead of Bacchus' beasts. Bitch-eyes, disdaining the altar and Marsyas' fate.

She has skin of iron. Inside there are machines
which hold the broken parts in place;
a lump of golden ore instead of brains
keeps its hope close behind the mask we call a face.
This nymph is not for pressing. Is there no membrane you could strip away

with a splitting tool? I'm trusting as a fool and too used
to your quiet pandemonium, your necromancer's ways, to question
your revolt, and wait it out till you drop your little guillotine,

working a tear between our dreams and the false starcrust
of this canvas. Oh, make a changing scene.

But the fly moved on oblivious to my rant,
because it knew what I did not want to believe
of the waste of this vocation: surface
is the opposite of flight, and all art *is* surface.

The Critic

No thanks to the credulous! It's clearly a woman.
Plainly, this is indicated by these two horns. The artist

is obviously some kind of satirist, a woman-hater
or hater of woman-haters - it's hard to say which.

You're not convinced? Look, these many-legged fossils
are her eyes, these breached cocoons her breasts,

and the black economy of his mind is grateful
for this tear in the fabric (or is it a stab in the dark?).

Artists can get away with anything. Did you know Hitler
painted? Yes, flowers as yielding to sight as ghosts,

under dreamy washes spires capped with crooked crosses,
veiled women and the infirm of step trembling under strokes.

Such a delicate hand.

Headcase

A headcase without a doubt.
Look, his dark pack with him,
a strange jolt from the knees,
the drag and tow of one ankle.

Mark his gait, his sway, the drift
of one eye. Poor stammerer.
Expressions open and close
before him. Vermin creep about

his feet. What are we to do
with him? And who knows
what goes on inside! Divide
and let him pass. There are

coiled worms ready in his lungs,
under his nails' tips; mood-eaters
hang on his clothes, and dwell
in the bag they use to drain

the fluids out. Distance alone
can save you. Human minds disdain
what monsters entertain. Keep him
thence and therefore love him.

PART 2: THE BOILER HOUSE GALLERY

This painter was to counterfeit the skirmish between the Centaurs and the Lapithes, and had been very desirous to see some notable wounds, to be able the more lively to express them… [T]he effect of blows… so amazed him that he stood stock still, while [a warrior]… strake off both his hands. And so the painter returned well skilled in wounds, but with never a hand to perform his skill.

— Sir Philip Sidney, *The Countess of Pembroke's Arcadia*, Book II

Greek's Blood Turk's Blood

Your disease took us by surprise.
For days your cells remained
in the chemist's wicked vials;
severed glass fingers, confounding
- with their labels of O and A -
Greek's blood Turk's blood Jew's DNA.

By what inscrutable alchemy he had turned
blood into death we could not tell,
but the writing was on the wall.
Now our words are small splayings. Your bitten lips
have made your mouth a ring of roses.

Visitors

> Words fail, there are times when even they fail… What is one to do then, until they come again?… so little to say, so little to do, and the fear so great, certain days, of finding oneself… left, with hours still to run, before the bell for sleep, and nothing more to say, nothing more to do...
> — Samuel Beckett, *Happy Days*, 1961

Those days when quiet
lifted a thought, gave it a heft
that could pass by you,
brushing an ear an elbow,
lifting invisible hairs on its way,
connecting what feels like
postponement to the one
unalterable concept of the brink.

Those days I thought of you
shrunk back, the puckered
interface of an amputation,
locked out of sounds, lips
to a pressure sore, trying
your desires in plosives. Please,
I'm saying I want your face
in my hands to stop this
flickering and oozing, as if
everything that's wrong
with the world pours through
the spaces in your expressions.

Those days, what happens to you
when even the visitors' words
are empty, when day-after-day
becomes a kind of possession,
hoarding under haematology
flecks of half-life-bullion,

jagged minerals, keen gold-leaf
and cutting-ore, that will become
the sticking places of tumours?

Eye Your Brother

She gropes for the roots of a word, finds 'more'
and pulls out 'morphine' (like a magician
breaking a wrist-watch under black cloth
then drawing out, in its place, a perfect dove).

Your bed is a city-wall defended
with treacherous parts, your ramparts
a museum of consequences. A silver liver
on its sling feeds itself from your blood,
and we are all 'visitors' who are not dying.

Only a dropped toy boat for one ecstatic
moment enters grief, severing 'child'
from 'visitor', and you have time to eye
the boy and eye your brother and, in-between

each drop of the drug, its slow-declining scale
on the monitor's monograph, set schedules
for ruling, reaping and return, you will only
keep in sleep but waking never firmly hold to oaths.
The room wobbles and wanes, pitches, pinches

a fixed point on the nurse's pillaging needle,
then stretches itself through the door, turning
our hopes inside out. The toy boat is blue, blue
as Caesar's robe, *et tu*, *et tu*, blue as Aurelia's eye.

The Buried House

There where you'd set your foot
on the buried house, the turf roof
gave, caved in. To whatever lay
inside, its unaccustomed eye

hauling shapes from the pitch,
the breach would have been
the uncoiling of a shuttered lens,
a surfacing ammonite crumbling

to an interlipped hoop, inviting light.
Surely it mapped the upperworld,
the life that it had never known,
in your scent, the peaks and valleys

of your cries as we played, not yet
in our teens, and had turned its craft,
its senses piqued, to the possession
of your immaculate topography.

So the buried house, or whatever
called it home, waited for you,
watching for the shadows of your
quick legs, tossing and recovering

light like an electric fan, as you ran
above the spyhole you had made,
knowing it would take only one slow step,
one stop, to catch and pull you under.

The Bone-Altar

Stooping over the basin,
your studied head a bruised peach,
inside not dense but sensing

stone, I'm sprained on an alien act
of worship. I think of
the frozen girls in the Andes,

caved and creeled in quiet,
their young breasts shrunk
to pitted olives, their ovaries

stolen. Somewhere, through ice
and annals the axeman's qualm
still speaks from their tainted brows.

How can pity stick to the past
like that? I know what I am holding.
Your hair slinks evasive as crude oil

through cracks in my thoughts.
I crane my neck to the bathroom mirror
and suddenly I am a bone-altar.

Shamed, I'm sure you have seen it:
the witch-doctor's sentence sits in my memory,
like votive light in a lamb's skull.

Wintering

We hewed a rough passage through
the quiet inclination of the wood.
Every tree I saw was you,
its pocked brown bones your body caked in mud,

no longer where we'd left it.
Trees have tongues, they tell our faults and laugh.
I've noticed a drowned bow split;
its snap was like your name, its crook a graph

of love. I've lost the reach
of this affair, that trigger for the match,
picked each slur like a leach,
wintering in, from skin too bruised to touch.

The Window

> We must be still and still moving
> Into another intensity
> For a further union, a deeper communion…
> — T.S. Eliot, 'East Coker', 1940, *Four Quartets*

What mystery is there
in bone that finds us
unprepared for work,
the way joints lock

as soft, not stone,
as soil on soil, when motion
is the confidante
of pain, and hardly suffers

standing, or when dead skin
accumulates a life,
how outside ourselves
we understand our loss?

All this I could explain.
But you were lawless.
With more than a hint
of the 'magic-brutal'

(a movement you invented)
you spoke a crazy
music and hated the tremor
of touch. When your limbs

revolted, your anger
could unapparel the sky, burn
a hole in the heart of starlight.
No-one could tell why

the room let go of its edges,
or you couldn't manage
the stairs; why the optic's
blue thunderbolt singed

the world you moved in; why
the skins inside you unknotted
their immaculate ribbons.
But you have time enough

to contemplate these things,
threadbone boy, skyrattler,
razer of ruined youth,
staring from your window.

The Boiler House

> Approach the chamber, and destroy your sight
> With a new Gorgon. Do not bid me speak –
> See, and then speak yourselves –
> — William Shakespeare, *Macbeth*, 2.3.73-75

In the boiler house at the end of the garden,
you would keep your face pressed against
the white gas-heater whole hours, waiting
for the blue flame to speak itself into life.

Then you'd see how long it would take
before you needed to tear your cheek away.
There are still scratches down the wall, following
the same arcing fall as a profiled rib-cage,

Holbein's tomb-laid Christ. And I can imagine
your fingers quarrelling with some edge
the way the dead God's hand, wired with rigor mortis,
gripped the cold stone shelf. You had to be

accustomed to the burn to make those Hell-Raiser
faces, those Krueger masks, for your paintings.
Screechgatherers, they were made to stare after
the pretty human trophies for which you'd hungered.

The Ring

He must also in this counterfeiting take heede of too much taunting in touching a man, especially in the ill favourednesse of visage, or ill shape of bodie. For as the mishaps and vices of the bodie minister many times ample matter to laugh at, if a man can discretely handle it, even so the using of this manner too bytingly, is a token not onely of a common jeaster, but of a plaine enemie.
— Baldassare Castiglione, *The Book of the Courtier*, 1528, trans. Thomas Hoby, 1561

It was not a mistake.
I saw them do it, saw
them pull away
your whole face,

like one of Gomorrah's
vulcanised obscenities,
and when they showed you
the cast you turned

into an angry god
and your mouth
was a hollow cut
in a bronze relief.

When the children
came to gibe at you
and stick pins
in your scalp, gawking

at the awkward way
your limbs twitched,
you carved
your own prehistory;

and it was the mask
you wore when they danced
in a ring around you.
Pitiless rites. Revenge

was your genius
to make them ask
if the mask was worse
than what it covered up.

That made me want
to put my head under too.
I was an amateur; hack-parer.
You perfected yourself

at the melting-point's liquidwork,
another Valhalla.
Now your face is a ring of light.
The children have stopped dancing.

The Chosen

They found you helpless, not yet
fashioned for dreaming, and without
wonder struck out the thousand
uncaught enchantments you could
have stored from star-columns,

sleeping lives on walls dense
with homunculi, the molten eyes
of river-toads, glistening shoal-gods,
touches sticky as swamp-rot,
loved as harkened bird-song.

All this they took, cool as priests, leaving
you pill-locked and sightless, hung short
of the fall that gave you the look
of an angel pushing through shrouds,
the contours of your face half-

surmised like bruises through the gauze,
and the terrible concave of your mouth,
its brutal grammar, miming to be
understood by anyone; just one. Year
after year they wheeled you back

muzzled after experiments; your eye-lids
chafed by the leather straps, hips
in a nailed corset, the shiny buckles
out-shaming the light's indignities,
a spiked tongue-depressor clasped

to your scold's bridle. You never complained.
I never could tell why, until now, realising
it was your way to make me succumb
to events as you wanted me to see them,
with the gift of a very precise horror

you held towards me like a sacrifice:
the snake in the skull's socket, the broken
temples, the rattle-tail with its promise
of voices, a mask with a bleeding eye;
and the venom you unleashed

was the antidote when it was they who
were dying. No, not a redeemer, nor
a revenger. Your fingers are shattered.
The double-helix of your art unspools
from your brain-stem and you swallow it

down. Suddenly you have broken through
the wrappings. You emerge biting.
Your head swings back like a visor, releasing
light and blinding lasers, carving
back with photons your paintings into their flesh.

Now they crawl. Now your enemies cannot touch you.

Believing the Canvas

By heaven, thou echo'st me
As if there were some monster in thy thought
Too hideous to be shown. Thou dost mean something…
Show me thy thought.
— William Shakespeare, *Othello*, 3.3.109-119

It wasn't that you'd raised your hand
or pulled my eye to arc with yours.
It wasn't that you'd cupped the sound
around the corners of my dreams.

As in a darkened room there's room
for instinct to fill in the void,
the slow atonement of your stare
drew out a horizontal line

from sex to death and back again
and stopped me asking what it meant.
You looked a brother into me
and cancered loss before it knew

itself to be the place of love.
You were a picture when you died
time and again before your time.
You staged for me a killing rhyme,

made now and never sound the same,
insisted on complicity
and made belief meet murder with
a smile that could upstage a god.

51

> Behold, I was shapen in iniquity… Make me to hear joy and gladness; that the bones which thou hast broken may rejoice… O Lord, open thou my lips…
> — Psalm 51, *King James Bible*, 1611

Black grain, black logolatry of earth,
the smooth cut throats of the wheat-shafts,
muttering back their strain in hymn,
through winds in prayer unwinged,
forgotten martyrs, *O saviour, save me*. Stop,
in perfect kindness so sharp-toothed,
stop here and worship with me,
where air and soil prove their kin in chemicals,

not like our human stratagems.
Those plucked-out eyes have not offended,
nor your tongueless mouth blasphemed,
those quivering hands uncontouring
desire, but with just a thought-word loosed,
Thou washest me whiter than snow,
God's promise inhabits every iota
of matter like spawning foetuses; you, not alpha,

not omega, shuffle on your legs'
broken galleries. But this will not stop you.
Like the careful spider, I catch everything
beyond your reach in my net of memories,
as if I can keep it all for you. We face the harvest.
The cutters are coming, and you are not to be touched.
I look through you and smile. Is this blood
in the loam or the beautiful glimmering of Buddha?

Roaming Signals

So, now go tell, and if thy tongue can speak,
Who 'twas that cut thy tongue and ravished thee...
Write down thy mind, bewray thy meaning so,
And if thy stumps will let thee, play the scribe.
— William Shakespeare, *Titus Andronicus*, 2.3.1-4

It was what might be termed a phase;
before you lost your voice,
you'd speak all night to no-one else,
and this went on for years.

With little time to spare you stayed
fretful and open-eyed,
mouthing through the gloom each word
that could never again be said

when whatever it was that bled
the heart out of your head
and laid your whole life on your bed
would stop the wordstream dead.

Every gasp cut from dialect's holy ghost,
was a pill you popped for its gist,
each vowel cupped around a host,
from the dark's teeth pressed

to your dark lips and weighed on the bone.
You had all your nights strung,
end to end, on the endless moan
that caved our dreams in,

your mutterings like messages
left on old mobile phones
unread, untracked by roaming signals
reading empty spaces.

Burl

> But a caged bird stands on the grave of dreams
> his shadow shouts on a nightmare scream
> his wings are clipped and his feet are tied
> so he opens his throat to sing.
> — Maya Angelou, *I Know Why The Caged Bird Sings*, 1969

We're twelve years in
and you've lost
even the hard click
of your palate,

the guttural burl
that connected
your curbed will
to a flask of water,
a bright green
commode, a rice-
cracker white
and hopeful as a
communion wafer.

Lipstark and jabber,
you unfurl your tongue
and it is sublime,
a Tibetan prayer-rag
loosed to the wind's
larceny and squander.
Suddenly every
thing in the world
is the capped scream
of your mouthings.

Pressure Sore

Less a ghost's kiss, more a breathstroke
to my inner ear, your visitation
in the heavy heart of night was a hauling back
from the unspoken hereafter of wounds

a memory which had laid itself like a saint's gift,
or graft, outside the shrine of kindled thought.
It was your first pressure sore: the archetype.
When we peeled back the gauze we saw

a tunnel of aged fumitory, *earthsmoke*,
funnelled through the flesh's circuit,
terminating in an irregular slab of bare bone,
a basalt door's promise of the volcanic cathedral

beyond. I had seen it before, a pinched and weeping
thing, a wattled eye staring back from a book
about your condition, and thought you'd never get one.
But the fear looked itself into your life and so

we packed it - they showed us how to coax in
congealed iodine and dressings threaded
with pure silver - and watched it turn itself
slowly inside out, layering in secret stations

its simulacra of committed tissue. We knew
this sham slip would never be the same as you.
It wasn't real DNA that pulsed codes
into your blood but the thick acrylic you'd used

in your works, the shining graphite that caked
each sketch you'd plied. Inside the sore you were keeping
the peacock-feather-eyes of innocents, tiger-skinned
flowers, the crucifixes made of village hands,

you could no longer draw on a dead field.
We knew, as sure as day follows day and wound
follows wound, you would turn, haled whole
through a living canvas-skin, into one of your paintings.

Other Wounds

> Now the relative immunity of the well-proportioned body to external influence is clear from the very fact of its good mixture... Such a body will automatically be endowed with the best humours of all, and will thus be better able to withstand grief, anger, insomnia, worry, rain, drought, plague, and indeed all causes of disease. It is ill-humoured bodies which most readily succumb to such things, since they are in themselves already near to a state of disease.
> — Galen, *The Best Constitution of Our Bodies*, trans. P. N. Singer, 1997

What you held pressed to your heart
was not the blade's point, not
the razor to the split-lip of skin
you always kept covered. There were,

in other words, other wounds. The sleeve
in which you'd slipped your body
was an alien graft. And, not knowing,
they'd ask you if you'd ever hurt yourself.

The proof, they'd said, was plainly there
in your paintings. But they did not see,
or did not want to believe, that beneath
the red nympholepsy of your art,

by which I mean the study of yourself -
or violence to yourself; it's the same thing -
there was this trembling, this perplexity
of nerve-ends and colours (synaptic bursts?).

Then men in white coats came and blasted
your image onto a darkened plate,
and there it was: every hue clean out-bled,
imprisoned forever in glass, and named disease.

The MRI Scan As Art

Wound me not with thine eye, but with thy tongue;
Use power with power, and slay me not by art.
— William Shakespeare, *Sonnet 139*

Its action is a bargain struck
between the nature of light

and the accomplishments
of collision. All vectors

and collapsing gridlines,
it reasons with atomic velocity,

thinking itself into textile, skinwork,
into the bare bones of event,

even hunting other human thoughts.
It opens eyes into everything

and its eyes are ovine, black points
on its graph of Chaos-theory.

Its gadolinium swirls bleed
little blossoms into your cerebellum.

Touched, neurons cough up
their voltages, myelins untrussing,

lipids, calcia, axons exploding
like stars; all your synaptic divinities

deriddled. In this nuclear winter
you'll sleep; your throat-cords

shrinking, till the love of flesh
for fission burns you down

to the hopeful nudity of an instant,
your jagged-self scarred

like an exposure on your rockbed.
Waking you will wonder how

you've raised such splendors,
such radiant art outside

yourself, as if your mind had
always toiled beside its own image.

Your 'Condition'

A sliver of tin perhaps, a fragment
of enamel, or a hoop of wire, wedged
somewhere in-between the crux

of vertebra and encephalon, poised
like a question between hard facts. What a joy
to be able to say 'This is the problem', to let

scalpel and pincer release your body
from complication, and to comprehend,
peering into the drift and gist of these relics,

that every termination of the valgus, flaw
in the cerebellum, elephantiasis, crank
neurosis, is nothing but the tangle of debris,

sharp, glittering, twisted among the living tissue.
And your eye against the glass, its smashed
schematics, the broken coils of nerve-yarns

through celestial iodine, are more cherished,
being drama to the infinite and impenetrable
trash upon which your 'condition' depends.

The Examination

It was they who unrooted
the raw world out of you,
rage and claw and ablution and all
those little spiked secrets,

heirs of bone and bacillus,
that bloomed inside you; you, as always
insisting on the incredibles of yourself,
kept from the vagaries of solution,

were tonged from familiarity's shell.
But they only wanted to examine
your mouth, the pulpy inside
of your cheek, the quiet click click

of your ear-bones, crack their oblique
morse-code, the miraculous shape
of your syllables. Hands crossed
over your chest, you made an effigy

of yourself. But they only wanted
to press the cells of your heart and watch
the arteries unkiss themselves
from your enigmas, their lips gasping

for air. Turning once I saw you biting
your flesh through the bars; their shadows
were scalpels to your delicacy.
You became the martyr you dreamed

upon the table. Gauze-skins were unzipped
to the bowing bones, bones shaved down
to their marrows, marrows desponged,
and dried, lifted in parcels to flaunt

nerves released from their sheaths
like electric wires exposing their charges
through plastic subways funnelled out,
connections broken, unearthed.

Their eyes are all spring and unchaste
flowering. Chasing their breaths,
they rise with your fall, never needing,
like me, the chance to keep your love whole.

Dead Reckoning

I, the performer…
masked by the table…
My wrist extended a scalpel…
I stand in the presence
of the destroyed god…
Knowing that the work is mine
how can I love you?
— Margaret Atwood, 'Speeches for Dr Frankenstein', *The Animals In That Country*, 1986

And there goes another piece.
A molar this time, then the ball
of cartilage that holds the jaw
in place. There's little skin left

to shroud the shameless proselyte
beneath. You have learnt the metre
of your disintegration, made
oenology of your body's fluids.

What common poverty inheres
is merely a dead reckoning
of the life that gathered itself
outside you. It is a safe bet,

the safest yet, that you, not flesh
but silica, breaking into sand,
will out-last even us, hoi polloi,
all stubborn mass and nastiness.

I won't insult your intelligence.
They feared you once, no longer,
when the devil in your look
was a magnetic storm that pulled

the air from their lungs, smashed
the vanity from their pretty faces,
stripping beauty from the bone.
My Merrick. Love. I won't forget.

Where Will You Stop?

This blood taboo is seen in numerous kinds of observances
which have nothing to do with sexuality...
— Sigmund Freud, *On Sexuality*

Craving again, we searched
for a way to pacify you
but something wingless
took hold of your stare,

occluding the miracle
we had come to expect
from smashed beanstalks,
a ball of fibres, fresh

minnows, or a bag
of roots; those we could cram
till the house was emptied
of ammunition. This once

you would not stop
at human skin; opening
and closing, you were
a pair of forceps,

pulling at a breech-birth.
Your teeth stuck
to our fingers. Satiety
was an event

you choreographed.
And you were a pro.
Till one day, we found you
like this; your voice quiet

as the shuffling of beetles,
abandoning panic
and the mystery of sex
to the blood and vision

of one fathomless question.

The Question

And can you by no drift of circumstance
Get from him why he puts on this confusion,
Grating so harshly all his days of quiet
With turbulent and dangerous lunacy?
— William Shakespeare, *Hamlet*, 3.1.1-4

Tell them
it's not the scars that they can see, not why
these melting sullied lumps of meat need engines,
bracing and choking contraptions, to coerce
them into the idea of a body they can love.

Tell them
it's because the world went dark the day they shone
a light inside you, and that's why your sleep
is not like death but like death's opposite,
a shambling thing born in an x-rayed heart.

Tell them
it's not the shocks of nature's renegades,
but the screaming cables in the flesh our voices
coil through that keeps you still described for us
within the brittle grammar of your silence.

Tell them
it's because you set a bone and gave the kiss
to save a traitor's life, who gave you back
that kiss again with his remaining fist,
that you punch holes through all your oppressors.

Tell them
it's not the will of action but its name
that is the peace that passeth understanding
and that's what we call history and why
the howler slips between its sickly pages.

And if they still want answers
then bite your tongue, and lift your mask, unloose
a thousand twisted images, to taunt
them with the monsters, golems, freaksters of your soul
their scorns, their whips, their laws cannot control.

The Feeders

If you were, after all, this mute Nostradamus
reading the bones of your fate,
then perhaps these apparitions were nothing more
than the broken pieces
of your own genetic code, loosed

from the hooks and helices which barbed them
beneath your then-still-human skin.
You were only a child - what, four or five? -
when the feeders came.

I don't suppose they ever challenged your logic
of the human arrangement
or its bloodied agreement with nature.
Perhaps, for you, attachment
was an unnecessary extravagance.

Body-parts could take on a life of their own,
could communicate, feed, and defecate
without the channeling of fluids in ducts and fleshy cylinders.

So ears lashed together, walking on their lobes' ends,
a species of Bosch-creation,
would twitch a garbled language
as they squeezed themselves into the unstopped bottles
on the drinks trolley,

and blood, not for you distinguishable from other organs,
would eat paint or suck the patterns from wall-paper
as it descended;

a gigantic, gelatinous stomach that would creep
towards you as you sat
cross-legged on the living-room floor.

All the time you were visited you were, you'd claimed, beset
by the familiar tinnitus of your childhood.
This would announce the feeders' entrance
like a kind of backing-track
and sound as long as the visions stayed.

Years later, when a different kind of ringing
took hold of your limbs
and made them dance, it was hard for me not to see
in each tic and judder the return of the feeders.
And your eyes, your feet, your throat-strings grew
to love their own volition,

hating your mind, hating the coherence of the fabric in your mind,
calving their own way

till

oh God, they had eaten you...

Walker

For you every step was a carnival. You wore
the idea of yourself in harlequin:
the mismatched patches of iodine swabs
and plaster-gauzes, the Russian-doll masks

of your funny-faces, and a proclivity to vanish
behind arras drawn smooth and blue
as a hospital bed's curtain. You made the children
dance to the pell-mell of your automaton clock-

work. Performing, you were a craft in neon,
a circus-tent for skin. You loved the curious
choreography of canned laughter, the sudden apocalypse
of event, the switch-blade-language of properties.

You embraced the literal in plastic: the implausibly
yellow banana-skins you winked at in your path,
the trick-carnation's squirts you excused
for your tears, guns firing 'Bang' to stop hearts

dead, the collapsible keg, and satires of bodily
functions. Your run had a story too. It taught us how
you learned to live without the gravity of flesh.
What was this naked being in earnest when

you quicksilvered at the pull of the tight-rope?
And how they cheered. Your encore was a stillness
that was all approximation, each limb baffled
in a probability of place, and the audience applauded

one last time. When you performed, my dear,
there was never an empty seat in the house.
What do they stare at now with such a hungered grace?
To whose show do they go when they can no longer

fever your thoughts with their looks? Who clowns his foot
for their amusement? But then there are the days
when in the dark of an unportraitured wall I see
a painted grin, shark-teeth, your eyes' deep hypnoscopes;

I hear again the arcade's song, the dank accordion,
the crude drum-roll before the freak comes on,
and I am overjoyed to feel your gloved hands reaching
through to catch and catch and clasp, shark-teeth gnashing.

Fossil

Fused between silt-crust and strata,

the pharmacopoeia of flesh bled clean,

you are a curled ammonite, an ancient

carbon ghost, kept shy of human ken

and hammer. Discovery now would

only destroy your pointed rivets,

your perfect horns, which measured

with their locked hand-in-fist, hand-

in-fist, the layering of time. So, near-keel,

you wait in the dark for the gentle

kiss of the ocean, the slow and lethal

kiss of the ocean, to reach you through

the crumbling walls of your silent land-vault.

Years slide out of sight. The rock-face

with its spoil of bone is being eaten away.

The Landfarer

> Then came wand'ring by
> A shadow like an angel with bright hair,
> Dabbled in blood and he shrieked out aloud…
> — William Shakespeare, *Richard III*, 1.4.49-51

I exhumed you once from the still side
of this tor. Your after-rain-skin smelt

like moss on granite-stone. Afraid
of wrecking the hulk I buried you again.

What is it keeps you lost? Is it the pills,
or has the meaning of your body changed?

In sleep, are you losing your dreams to mere
alterations in air-pressure (those easily mistaken

for the clear elevations of music)? Do the stars,
for you, still pulse with their cast-iron trust,

or have they become bleeding fissures
in the smote pelt of space? I've noticed you

struggling into steps like the lately born.
You have outgrown your own industry

and know yourself for a landfarer. I promise you
some day they will discover a white scar

on the face of this hill. They will ask questions
of the withered legs, the pretty broken pinions,

the feathers' cuneiform still pressed into the soil.
They will come to realise, by these tokens,

fools, the smallness of what uttered paradise
they have fathomed, now or in history, taken

for the one and only unalterable truth: that beauty
belongs to the beck of angels not to the unsound.

Lip-Reader

When you were 'unsound', when your thoughts
were a bag of bones you dragged to drown out, out-sound,
other breathers, your mind's penumbra cast

their vast primeval silhouettes against the walls
of the house that ate you. You dressed them in skin
and sorries, till they were familiar with limits and the freight

of hunger. Little sacks inside began to pump, pushing
fundamentals through. Clever you, Prometheus-clever.
You learned to act as if they were not there at all, losing

with intent my voice's androgens. I spoke, but my words
stuck, like wet petals you could hardly peel away. Memory did not do,
no, not for you philology's guesswork, but matter

mattered. It was not in memory they resumed the old trick
of sounding true. It was in the fabric, in the thrum of a crowded field.
Of course! You'd lost the shape of words before the diagnosis. Lines

of dye and graphite spoke, art hatched through with hurt. Fifteen years
later, when you started seeing them again (or forging them -
what difference could there be?), we all thought you were losing

your mind. A fresh scar or a tooth-print, any small protrusion,
would have set the record straight, would have proved braille
to our oblivious fingers. But you were clean and uncomplicated

as a full-term baby. Then one day we became the ghosts
and canvases had lungs. You said something bitumen-mouthed, disgorging
your explanations. I squinted closer. I think I saw my name.

Anything But You

...then you returned
with that carnival smile
you had perfected, all
these years, from ear to ear
embellishing a death-mask.

This you could, with the slightest
pinch of affectation, maul
to a kind of vapour, or seen
as lightning through a cloud,
become a relief in negative,

an x-ray's furious aura, hostile
to even my idolatry. You tore
strips off the cheeks of those
who offended you, bit morsels
out of their assurance. Now

the streets where you walked
are quiet as heaven, the rooms
in which you painted full
with cubits of your measurable
absence in my mind-maps

of your spaces. You want
to speak my wide thoughts
through a tracheotomy;
but my words are wedged
like coins I have to dive for,

breaking into membranes made
from fossil-oils, in an ocean-bed's
impossible plush and furl.
You are a hoard, your chest
a sea-chest raided by dead coral,

the commerce of enzymes
arrested from gold sucked clean
of its rudiments. My eyes
are hostages to this sacrifice.
Is this what they call a ransom,

an offering? But you out-stare
my theology, my theoria, god of blades
and hammerblasts, the scourge
of the prettyskins, an accidental
wreaker. My fingers test empty air

before I plunge them in; hands returning
with precious useless wires, a crust
formed from atrophied brain-stem,
the hope that turns a drug into a totem,
all that can be anything but you.

Another Year

It was getting harder and harder to tell.
When you choked and guttered,
when your jaw locked with the wale
of some unswallowable thing,
panic seized the strings of my throat.

When your eyes were monoliths
that would not balk erosion,
I squinted to discover the hieroglyphs
in their keeping. Seasons passed
and I could no longer distinguish

your limbs from mine, your insomnia
from my carefulness to intercept
the first tremoring of need. Oh Father
is this what incarnation is like:
volition as the unfamiliar aggregate

of densities? Are there no limits,
no hard edges to interrupt
this wilderness? Parables come
so unfalteringly: *perhaps it won't*
be so bad this year, perhaps it will.

Curating A Life

But if there be nor ever were one such,
It's past the size of dreaming. Nature wants stuff
To vie strange forms with fancy...
— William Shakespeare, *Antony and Cleopatra*, 5.2.95-7

The bare shapes of these bodies
would have turned our memories
into dead geometry without this lung-
valued scattering of lustres into open

air, this river collecting itself in spirals
beyond the wade and muzzle
of the landbank. The day laid
its charities at your feet, but you

had no mind for its running
sea-shelves, for the gulls
that tracked the skyborne
cartography of their own cries

till they encountered solids.
The gluttony of the moon
 - it bit at the dark -
had nothing to do with love,

the cicada knew no oratory,
the cliff was no dissolved monastery,
and you scoffed at the could-or-
could-nots of sweethearts.

So you stored up your own stories,
peopled world upon world
with strange, jittery forms,
barely machinery to opulence

and flesh; not hourly-promised
alternatives to breath, but
breathings of a braver life,
where beauty didn't matter.

One day I found you regarding
a painting, still dripping. You asked,
shall I tear it? Bored (this again!),
I blurted, will that make it better?

Two days later I came across
a fragment neatly placed
against my pillow's headless crook,
to my curator scored on the back.

I keep it still, though faded now,
in a book of unprinted verse,
closed in a draw, with the backgifted
cufflinks that you never wore.

The Possession

You've not taken to spitting raw cuts and coal,
brass pins and wire elements. Here's no satanic
yoga, nor machinery of thrown voices. You've slid

into possession the way a seagull finds its furrow
in the slipstream, inhabiting the drift of the earth's
habitual needs. Your possession is not an invasion.

(Keep it quiet. This is our secret). It turns the light-bulb
into a muscle pumping photons into your external
organs, keeping here a commode alive, there a pack of pills

breathing, knotting your nerve-ends to your bed.
The thermometer on the wall is a silver gland, endlessly
swallowing and secreting against the hard fever

of the world; and your face is now a wholesome swirl
of rootless stems and seeds, now a voodoo mask crumbling
with wood-rot and worm, betraying no trace, no human

memorandum, of anything you need to love. Brother
I have learned so much. How can I thank you
for your possession which transforms me still still still?

The Other Side of the Wall

Child, your sins are forgiven.
It was that easy. Then the pull
of the rope, the flourish of feathers
and stubborn beaks in tree-tops. Cut free,
in free-fall, the lung's collision with air.
Someone's lips are moving in prayer,

then in wonder, and suddenly
you are sacred. Men in white robes
come and piece you together.
They anoint your wounds with oil.
And you are left outside the city gates
as the dark slips down like melted lead.

Hooded lepers and shortened children
on trolleys shuffle towards you, holding
wooden bowls. A pale and penitent concept
of woman with baby opens her hand.
This is the place where they are taken:
the bodies made too perfect by their first

deaths, the other side of the wall, crossed
only by the collectors of relics, hungry
to complete themselves with a lock of hair,
a clipped earlobe, a sock of flesh to hinge
to a stump, char of bone and scalp. You bleed
to bless them. My fingers stretch to catch a scrap.

Rough Medicine

When it wants to hurt, it will raise a tail,
stinging,
plunge a black syringe into your flesh,
sending
its poisoned sugar-compounds,
hissing
into your nervestream. A pearl of blood

will congeal in seconds, tight little bud,
sealing
the busy toxin in, till antibodies facsimile
hurting
to heal it. To hit on it, you need only think of
lip-sewing
Olmec, their offerings interred in leather bags;

preserved in their eternal crash-positions,
hiding
inside the exact distillation of themselves,
gathering
a gradual panacea for the body's debt to gravity.
Pounding
the residue to powder, men with moonstones set

in their pitted teeth will burn and gift it to the spiritless,
tearing
a window in the Jaguargod's wide skypitch.
Playing
there their Ulama, the 'life-death' game (the whole race
taking
from thence its name), there will be no more losing.

So between our souls there is a ribbon of arsenic,
working
our prayers' rough medicine into remedial scars.
Taking
into my hands your labours, each sweatdrop precious, worth
stealing,
like annealed mercury, I let you sting and sting again.

Crane Fly

I tried to forget the crane fly
underneath your flesh,
wedged somewhere in the brain's
stem, cranial incubator, her wings
of spilt petrol's potential refraction,
though hedged in dark,
embracing dura mater, in inaction
sensing synaptic sparks.

But whenever she fluttered
your eye became skewed
on an invisible sightline,
your hands retraced every lost
motion they had ever made,
and needs formed pleading
little lips of spittle on your lips
too hushed to be heeded.

Her haste was a mother's haste
to hatch her clutch, unspool
the school in her thorax.
Beyond the breathing
of my waking thoughts, I heard
the crane fly's happy ending:
the shimmering flight to freedom,
the fathering shell of you broken.

The Final Hour

> And so as long as the mind makes proper use of the organs of the body it is called sane and healthy, but once it begins to break its bonds and tries to win freedom, as if it were planning an escape from prison, men call it insane. If this happens through disease or some organic defect, by general consent it is called insanity... I think this also explains why those who are struggling at the hour of death often have a somewhat similar experience, so that they speak wonders as if inspired.
>
> — Desiderius Erasmus, *Praise of Folly*, 1511, trans. Betty Radice, 1971

It was easy to imagine you
skulking through the thick;
some unchained thing,
terrible amnesiac.

Mined and hollow of voices,
plosive as a dagger,
you were half a heart-
beat at the heart of nothing

in your brother's heart.
Around you I became
the embellished horns
and sickles of a vortex,

the light's last I.O.U.s
propelled to their singularity.
You were an alchemist.
I was your Blood-King.

After the experiment failed,
I had to re-organise
your charrings. I put you
on display. Children came

and peered into the pits
that were left. Your rocked
body was a lullaby, the tips
of your fingers molten ore. I saw

a hardly-believable concave
for a face, symmetry-appalled.
And I was grateful you had made it,
because you gave it to me.

Beyond the cleaving your hunger
tore right through the paintings
in your boiler house. The pigment spun
into spray, the sitters' eyes bubbling up,

composed smiles blistering, necks
smiling canvas teeth, the canvases
unlooping fibres scraped
into breathable dust. Inhaling,

after the final hour, I hold
your head in my arms and study
the gorge. I push my thumb
inside. I ask, but you clam up.

History

Once you came back in a dream or such bodework.
Your face was big and white, a heron's bright wing
caught in a tree-snare. My teeth were seamed
to your hair and I was a Norse warrior pulling
the histories of the dead from a brass spirit-bowl.

We're hacked-through with Valhalla Valhalla Valhalla.
I'm scared of these signs. All histories cut both ways.

Sea-Rites

At last we touched upon the lonely shore
  that never yet has seen its waters sailed
  by one who then returned to tell the tale.
— Dante, *The Divine Comedy: Purgatory*, trans. Mark Musa, 1981, Canto 1, ll. 130-32

Let Love clasp Grief lest both be drown'd…
— Alfred Tennyson, *In Memoriam A.H.H.*, 1850, I.9

It is hard to make sense
of this light, its frivolous
terrestrial sweep over
the black heaplands, its lick

and furrow windward.
And I am never more sorry
for the blood it raised
to your eyes, and the hazard

of its honesty, unlayering pitch
from jagged face. It is late,
and the tides have made
their mournful retreat, dragging,

bowed and back-scuttling,
their long salty hair over the shingles
and sand-slates. Your hands have
forgotten all their seizures,

your possessions ghost-eased into
fading fingermarks. Under what spoor
and puzzle of the shore shall I
bury this vast hoard of love?

A Work in Progress

I want to keep you
held between
the boy who painted
horrors passing
through their softer selves
till they felt like comforts,

and the young man
whose trembling carried on
into the room,
into the lives in that room,
into the world around those lives,
when he stopped trembling.

Now I know what sums this up,
in this room, on this bed
where you lay
keeping our lives from folding in.
Though you are dead love
is a work in progress, still being made.

How can I say

you are dead
when simply saying
so you pulse

into view, a bio-
luminescent
scavenger caught

in the lights
of a submerged hub,
x-rayed

to your articulate
bones the way
my fingers

read you, living,
when the teeth
and tentacles

beneath your skin,
as I washed
and dressed you,

fed me with
poison I felt for
love?

The Beast

There would this monster make a man – any strange beast there makes a man.
— William Shakespeare, *The Tempest*, 2.1.30-31

O taste and see… all that lives
to the imagination's tongue… transform
into our flesh…
— Denise Levertov, 'O Taste and See', *O Taste And See*, 1964

You were a Fauve, *excellentissime domine*,
one of the beasts.
You never uttered in earnest
what you could show to burn,
reducing elements
for flint in the crucible of your mortality.

When you put your hand to them,
sun-sharer,
ordinary events became radiant stratagems
in cinnamons and oxides.

And so whenever you relapsed, it was to a world
where nothing slept,
nothing simply reposed. From the gargantuan cypress
to the tanned wrists of village-dwellers in Famagusta,
you translated the linear,
freeing them from the ageless run
of systems, from the vibrations in nerves, and the arrangement

of thresholds. Loving, you poured things out of themselves
in coils and kamikaze spirals, squeezed
glutinous as amber-tar, or thick gum arabic:
the molten-gold faces of hopeful children,
balloon-like women, opulent and perfectly guilty of satieties,
the foaming nectar shaken from strange blooms
over the shoulders of lovers.

Outside the frame-work hunger can be explained,
you seemed to be saying,
if you are prepared to consider
the puzzle of bone without the pristine schematics we are sold as nature;

something touchable you can wrap up and fold away
in an old leather case or a dresser drawer,
and produce at a moment's notice, pin to the wall, lay on the floor, drape over a chair-back or bed,
when visitors call round and you have a mind to hospitality
or when it's time to tell your story.

You seemed to be saying, other sacrifices are unnecessary.
Only give up the ghost of language. Cease
the struggle after new voices, and live in colour,
from mute room to mute room, failing no-one's flesh, failing no-one's wisdom.

To know your hands are never empty, is to taste
your own completion.

Then you will open, then you will bleed and see.

On Gratitude

Are you angry? What a thing to ask me on your anniversary.
And in truth, where was it now, all that ferocity of feeling?

Plunging a hand into the wound I pulled out an alien root.
I replanted it, loved it, watched its bloodflower bloom,

named it Gratitude; not for your pain, your too-young-death
(I want you living still, no matter the cost to you,

which is I know a selfish wish), but for what I grasped
in your honour. This is a kind of warcreed, a warrior-code,

the success you made of your life because you made it
your way, even while your body betrayed you at every turn.

I knew you'd say that, he replied, beaming. No matter how
abridged the life, love makes loss a conquest, a reclamation.

I Am Your Brother

My death was a quantity.
It filled me in stages.
I was a witch, a cutter, a queen,
I was your brother.

I'm sure you loved me
for you left me secret offerings
like I was a Tamarind spirit-tree,
hanging tooled autopsies,
glass eyes, and baby-shoes

from my dry branches.
When they laid me out,
they marvelled at my maternity.
My heart was an amniotic bag.

A self-embracing thing
still moved inside. You see,
I never lost myself completely;
though I was a burial, a terrorist,
a mask, I am your brother.

Bibliography

Works cited in the Introduction

Anon., *The true report of the forme and shape of a monstrous childe, borne at Muche Horkesleye* (1562), British Library, Huth Ballads

Anon., *The Forme and Shape of a Monstrous Childe, borne at Maydstone in Kent* (1568), British Library, Huth Ballads

Ashworth, Peter D., 'Seeing oneself as a carer in the activity of caring: Attending to the lifeworld of a person with Alzheimer's disease', *International Journal of Qualitative Studies on Health and Well-being*, Vol. 1, No. 4 (2006), pp. 212-25

Bacon, Francis, *Novum Organum*, *The Works of Francis Bacon*, ed. James Spedding (London: Longman and Co., 1875)

Bailey, Catherine, Romi Jones, Sue Tiplady, Isabel Quinn, Jane Wilcockson and Amanda Clarke, 'Creative writing and dementia care: making it real', *International Journal of Older People Nursing*, Vol. 11 (2016), pp. 244–54

Bolas, Helen, Anna Van Wersch and Darren Flynn, 'The well-being of young people who care for a dependent relative: An interpretative phenomenological analysis', *Psychology and Health*, Vol. 22, No. 7 (2007), pp. 829-50

Cachia, Amanda, 'The (Narrative) Prosthesis Re-Fitted: Finding New Support for Embodied and Imagined Differences in Contemporary Art', *Journal of Literary and Cultural Disability Studies*, Vol. 9, No. 3 (2015), pp. 247-49

Clarke, Steve, 'Where have all the disabled people gone?', 11 April 2017, https://rts.org.uk/article/where-have-all-disabled-people-gone

Davidson, Michael, *Concerto for the Left Hand: Disability and the Defamiliar Body* (Ann Arbor: University of Michigan Press, 2008)

Davis, Lennard J., *Bending over Backwards: Disability, Dismodernism, and Other Difficult Positions* (New York and London: New York University Press, 2002)

Davis, Lennard J., ed., *The Disability Studies Reader* (London: Taylor & Francis Group, 2016)

Day, Ally, 'Chronic Poetics, Chronic Illness: Reading Tory Dent's HIV Poetry through Disability Poetics and Feminist Bioethics', *Journal of Literary and Cultural Disability Studies*, Vol. 11, No. 1 (2017), pp. 83-98

Happell, Brenda, Karen Wilson, Chris Platania-Phung and Robert Stanton, 'Physical health and mental illness: listening to the voice of carers', *Journal of Mental Health*, Vol. 26, No. 2 (2017), pp. 127-133

Hobgood, Allison P., and David Houston Wood, *Recovering Disability in Early Modern England* (Ohio State University Press, 2013)

Hodges, Caroline E.M., Lee-Ann Fenge and Wendy Cutts, 'Challenging perceptions of disability through performance poetry methods: the *Seen but Seldom Heard* project', *Disability & Society*, Vol. 29, No. 7 (2014), pp. 1090-1103

Kuppers, Petra, 'Performing Determinism: Disability Culture Poetry', *Text and Performance Quarterly*, Vol. 27, No. 2 (2007), pp. 89-106

Kuppers, Petra, 'Scars in Disability Culture Poetry: Towards Connection', *Disability & Society*, Vol. 23, No. 2 (2008), pp. 141-50

Kuppers, Petra, 'Poetry-ing: Feminist Disability Aesthetics and Poetry Communities', *English Language Notes*, Vol.49, No. 2 (2011), pp. 73-82

Kuppers, Petra, 'Trans-Ing Disability Poetry at the Confluence', *Transgender Studies Quarterly*, Vol. 1, No. 4 (2014), pp. 605-13

Laoutaris, Chris, *Shakespearean Maternities: Crises of Conception in Early Modern England* (Edinburgh: Edinburgh University Press, 2008)

Loftis, Sonya Freeman, *Shakespeare and Disability Studies* (Oxford: Oxford University Press, 2021)

Love, Genevieve, *Early Modern Theatre and the Figure of Disability* (London: Arden, 2019)

McCarthy, Grace, *Shakespearean Drama, Disability, and the Filmic Stare* (London and New York: Routledge, 2021)

Mitchell, David T., and Sharon L. Snyder, *Narrative Prosthesis: Disability and the Dependencies of Discourse* (Ann Arbor: University of Michigan Press, 2000)

Nielsen, Emilia, 'Chronically Ill, Critically Crip?: Poetry, Poetics and Dissonant Disabilities', *Disability Studies Quarterly*, Vol. 36, No. 4 (2016)

Price, Margaret, 'Defining Mental Disability', in *The Disability Studies Reader*, ed. Lennard J. Davis (London: Taylor & Francis Group, 2016)

Pulman, Andy, Les Todres and Kathleen Galin, 'The Carer's World: An interactive reusable learning object', *Dementia*, Vol. 94, No. 4 (2010), pp. 535-47

Rogers-Shaw, Carol, 'Enhancing empathy and understanding of disability by using poetry in research', *Studies in the Education of Adults*, Vol. 53, No. 2 (2021), pp. 184-203

Sawday, Jonathan, *The Body Emblazoned: Dissection and the Human Body in Renaissance Culture* (London and New York: Routledge, 1995)

Shakespeare, Tom, 'Cultural Representation of Disabled People: Dustbins of Disavowal?', *Disability & Society*, Vol. 9, No. 3 (1994), pp. 283-99

Thomson, Rosemarie Garland, *Extraordinary Bodies: Figuring Physical Disability in American Culture and Literature* (New York: Columbia University Press, 1997)

Traub, Valerie, 'The Nature of Norms in Early Modern England: Anatomy, Cartography, *King Lear*', *South Central Review*, Vol. 26, No. 1/2 (2009), pp. 42-81

Tsiokou, Katerina, 'Body Politics and Disability: Negotiating Subjectivity and Embodiment in Disability Poetry', *Journal of Literary and Cultural Disability Studies*, Vol. 11, No. 2 (2017), pp. 205-222

Vincent-Connolly, Phillipa, *Disability and the Tudors: All the King's Fools* (Yorkshire: Pen & Sword, 2021)

Williams, Katherine Schaap, *Unfixable Forms: Disability, Performance, and the Early Modern English Theater* (Ithaca: Cornell University Press, 2021)

Intertexts and Works cited as Epigraphs to the Poems

Acosta, Joseph, *The Natural and Moral History of the Indies* (London: 1590)

Angelou, Maya, *I Know Why The Caged Bird Sings* (1969) (London: Virago, 1984)

Atwood, Margaret, 'Speeches for Dr Frankenstein', *The Animals In That Country* (1986), *Margaret Atwood: Eating Fire, Selected Poetry 1965-1995* (London: Virago, 1998 [2000 edition])

Bacon, Francis, *Novum Organum* (1620), *Francis Bacon: A Critical Edition of the Major Works*, ed. Brian Vickers (Oxford: Oxford University Press, 1996)

Basset, Robert, *Curiosities: or The Cabinet of Nature* (London: 1637)

Beckett, Samuel, *Happy Days* (1961) (London: Faber and Faber, 1961 [1966 edition])

Blagrave, Joseph, *The Astrological Practice of Physick* (London: 1671)

Browne, Thomas, 'Letter to William Dugdale', *On a bone dug from a cliff* (October 1660), *Sir Thomas Browne: Selected Writings*, ed. Claire Preston (Manchester: Carcanet, 2003)

Burton, Robert, *The Anatomy of Melancholy* (1621), *The Anatomy of Melancholy: A Selection*, ed. Kevin Jackson (Manchester: Carcanet, 2004)

Castiglione, Baldassare, *The Book of the Courtier* (1528), trans. Thomas Hoby (1561), ed. J. H. Whitfield (London: J.M. Dent and Sons, 1975)

Dante, *The Divine Comedy: Purgatory*, trans. Mark Musa, (Harmondsworth: Penguin, 1981 [1985 edition])

Donne, John, *A sermon preached at Whitehall* (8 April 1621), *John Donne: A Critical Edition of the Major Works*, ed. John Carey (Oxford: Oxford University Press, 1990)

Eliot, T. S., 'East Coker' (1940), *Four Quartets, T. S. Eliot: Collected Poems, 1909-1962* (London: Faber and Faber, 1963 [2002 edition])

Erasmus, Desiderius, *Praise of Folly* (1511), trans. Betty Radice (Harmondsworth: Penguin, 1971 [1993 edition])

Frazer, Sir James, *The Golden Bough* (1922) (Hertfordshire: Wordsworth Editions, 1993)

Freud, Sigmund, *On Sexuality*, ed. Angela Richards (Harmondsworth: Penguin, 1991)

Galen, 'The Best Constitution of Our Bodies', *Galen: Selected Works*, trans. P. N. Singer (Oxford: Oxford University Press, 1997)

Hildegard of Bingen, *The Book of Life's Merits, Hildegard of Bingen: Selected Writings*, trans. Mark Atherton (Harmondsworth: Penguin, 2001)

Levertov, Denise, 'O Taste and See', *O Taste And See* (1964), *Denise Levertov: New Selected Poems,* ed. Robert Creeley (Northumberland: Bloodaxe Books, 2003)

Locke, John, *An Essay Concerning Human Understanding* (1689), ed. Peter H. Nidditch (Oxford: Oxford University Press, 1979)

More, Thomas, *Utopia* (1516), trans Paul Turner (Harmondsworth: Penguin, 1965)

Morrison, Toni, *Playing in the Dark: Whiteness and the Literary Imagination* (London: Picador, 1992 [1993 edition])

Nilsson, Lennart, embryological photographs, *Life* magazine (30 April 1965)

Ovid, *Metamorphoses*, trans. Mary Innes (Harmondsworth: Penguin, 1955)

Palissy, Bernard, *Discours Admirables* (1580), trans Henry Morley (London: Chapman and Hall, 1855)

Pater, Walter, *The Renaissance* (1873), ed. Adam Phillips (Oxford: Oxford University Press, 1986 [1998 edition])

Plath, Sylvia, *Ariel* (London: Faber and Faber, 1965 [1968 edition])

Psalm 51, *King James Bible* (1611)

Quarles, Francis, *Hieroglyphics of the Life of Man* (London: 1638)

Shakespeare, William, *Antony and Cleopatra*, ed. John Wilders (London: Arden Shakespeare, 1995)

Shakespeare, Shakespeare, *Hamlet*, ed. G. R. Hibbard (Oxford: Oxford University Press, 1994)

Shakespeare, William, *King Lear*, ed. R. A. Foakes (Surrey: Arden Shakespeare, 1997)

Shakespeare, William, *Macbeth*, ed. Nicholas Brooke (Oxford: Oxford University Press, 1994)

Shakespeare, William, *A Midsummer Night's Dream*, ed. Peter Holland (Oxford: Oxford University Press, 1995)

Shakespeare, William, *Othello*, ed. E. A. J. Honigmann (Surrey: Arden Shakespeare, 1997)

Shakespeare, William, *Richard III*, ed. John Jowett (Oxford: Oxford University Press, 2000)

Shakespeare, William, 'Sonnet 139', *Shakespeare's Sonnets*, ed. Katherine Duncan-Jones (Surrey: Arden Shakespeare, 1997)

Shakespeare, William, *The Tempest*, ed. Stephen Orgel (Oxford: Oxford University Press, 1987 [1994 edition])

Shakespeare, William, *Titus Andronicus,* ed. Jonathan Bate (London: Arden Shakespeare, 2003)

Shakespeare, William, *Twelfth Night*, eds. Roger Warren and Stanley Wells (Oxford: Oxford University Press, 1995)

Sibbes, Richard, *A Fountain Sealed: or, The duty of the sealed to the Spirit* (London: 1637)

Sidney, Sir Philip, *The Countess of Pembroke's Arcadia*, ed. Maurice Evans (Harmondsworth: Penguin, 1987)

Tennyson, Alfred, *In Memoriam A.H.H.* (1850), *In Memoriam, Maud and Other Poems*, ed. John D. Jump (London: Everyman, 1995)

Whitney, Isabella, 'To her Brother. B.W.', from *A Sweet Nosgay* (1573), *Isabella Whitney, Mary Sideny and Aemilia Lanyer: Renaissance Women Poets*, ed. Danielle Clarke (Harmondsworth: Penguin, 2000)

Acknowledgements

This was a difficult book to write and probably even harder to show to others. I am grateful to so many who offered advice and feedback on the collection, who supported and encouraged me throughout its composition, and who played a part in my development as a poet. I would like to thank Aaron Kent at Broken Sleep Books for taking on this project so enthusiastically and sensitively, and for really 'getting it'. It is an honour to be published by a pioneering press which does so much good for local communities: a press with a heart. I have drawn tremendous inspiration from dear friends (in no order other than alphabetically!) Yasmin Arshad, Paul Edmondson, Anita Garfoot, Helen Hackett, Rowan Mackenzie, Vicky McMahon, Shona McNeill, Yewande Okuleye, Patricia Phillippi, Eleni Pilla, John Sutherland, and René Weis, who have energised and inspired my poetical and creative endeavours over the years, in many instances during the period in which most of these poems were written. I would like to thank Kathryn Moncrief for her belief in this project since the beginning, and Jehanne Dubrow for her valuable commentary and feedback on the poems at an early stage; their encouragement has been vital to the fate of this book in more ways than I have room to detail here. I am incredibly indebted (again, simply listed alphabetically here) to Sally Bayley, James Byrne, Katharine Craik, Neal Hall and Luke Kennard for their tremendous support and inspirational comments about my work; it means more than they could know. I owe special thanks to the Society of Authors and the judges of the Eric Gregory Poetry Awards for shortlisting this collection; this gave me the courage not to let go of these poems, but to keep on nurturing them even through periods when I resisted publishing them. I am very grateful to the *Parikiaki* newspaper, for which I produced work for a weekly poetry column during an early phase in this book's creation. Writing to tight deadlines was a hugely beneficial discipline and I am pleased that so many of my poems found a home in this newspaper, which has always supported my career and projects over the years. I am grateful to my colleagues at both University College London and The Shakespeare Institute (University of Birmingham) who provided supportive and enriching environments for my writing. I could not have written a word without the encouragement and love of my parents, Thalia and John, and without my brother, George, who is the fount of my creativity and has determined the way I see the world in so many ways. George, the lessons you have taught me are the greatest gift. I hope that through all my endeavours something of that gift is passed on to others. Thanks bro!!

LAY OUT YOUR UNREST

www.ingramcontent.com/pod-product-compliance
Lightning Source LLC
Chambersburg PA
CBHW070153100426
42743CB00013B/2896
* 9 7 8 1 9 1 5 0 7 9 9 0 9 *